All good wish from
HOOVER BOOTS and
MADAM
Audrey Hurry.

Hoover

Who Said Cats Can't Talk?

by

H. Boots

New Millennium
310 Kennington Road, London SE11 4LD

The Author wishes to state that this story is based on
fact but liberally sprinkled with fiction!

Any misrepresentation of human beings is entirely
accidental and the Author offers apologies to those who may
be offended.

Printed and bound by B.W.D. Ltd. Northolt, Middx.
Issued by New Millennium *
ISBN 1 85845 019 5
* An imprint of The Professional Authors' & Publishers' Association

To Derek Hurry
for all his help and encouragement.

Contents

Foreword

The stories contained in Who Said Cats Can't Talk are based on true incidents. Since the episodes are related by one of the cats appearing in the stories, they have been presented in a fictional manner.

H. BOOTS, otherwise known as **HOOVER**, sets down the stories as instructed by **MARMALADY**, a very elderly but arrogant lady-cat, who is annoyed by the attitude of some cat owners who enthuse over their pets without really understanding them! Both she and Hoover are convinced felines are superior and consider most humans to be somewhat troublesome, who do and say things, which to the feline mind have no rhyme or reason.

However, SIR, MADAM and ANDREW could be the exception that proves the rule, since they treat cats as friends and know they are 'owned' by them. The FAMILY, according to Hoover, understand that while cats do not have access to human speech, they are quite capable of making their feelings and needs known by different methods of communication, and by their behaviour, can indicate that they have understood, only too well, what humans have said.

Hoover discovers that the task he's been set has more problems than he bargained for, but luck plays its part and eventually he has nearly all the information he needs about the nineteen cats the FAMILY have 'owned' as pets over the years. He discovers whilst listening to a conversation when ANDREW gives MADAM a present that in actual fact there have been twenty cats who have played their part in MADAM's life.

Throughout the stories Hoover shows that the relationship between cat and cat is very like that between human and human and that in all societies, human or animal, someone has to be 'in charge'! He also tries to show that no two cats are alike; each has its own character, likes and dislikes.

Finally, Marmalady, the cat who presented Hoover with his task, succumbs to an infection; she has been with the FAMILY for nineteen years, so was certainly more than 90 human years old. Hoover feels that, although there are other stories he could tell, it's time to pause and think. Time for those who are left to pay their last respects to Marmalady, who couldn't be No. 1 because she was a lady-cat; but who, with feline wisdom, had provided for so many years the knowledge, guidance and care they had all needed.

If Only Cats Could Talk!

I used to lead a quiet, peaceful, uneventful life until the day Marmalady stalked into the living-room, tail swishing from side to side. Since then it's been nothing but hard work!

Marmalady was clearly very angry.

"What's the matter, M'lady?" I asked, quite expecting to be told to mind my own business.

"Can't talk indeed! It's enough to make a cat laugh!" Marmalady bristled with indignation. "If I hear another human say, 'it's a pity cats can't talk,' I shall set up such a caterwauling I shall be heard from here to Timbuctoo!"

I could understand how she felt. "What's upset you?"

"The lady with the Siamese from down the lane. She's been talking to MADAM about how clever her cat is even though it can't talk! Of course we don't talk as humans do, why should we? And when you think about it, there's usually too much human talk as it is."

Marmalady's attitude showed how offended she was.

"Well, there's not much you can do about it, M'lady. You know how silly some humans are. Why not treat such remarks with your usual contempt?" I watched Marmalady and I didn't like the thoughts I could sense passing through her mind.

"You, Hoover, will do something about it."

"But, M'lady ..."

"No buts, Hoover, you will set down all you know about how we came to be with MADAM, SIR and ANDREW - about those of us who are here now and those who have gone before."

I gazed at her in astonishment! Set down what I know about the FAMILY's cats? Where was I supposed to go for information about the nineteen cats that had lived with them

3

over the years?

"You will explain, to the best of your ability, that we have our own methods of communication which have served us well for years. People who like cats and understand them know we don't need human talk."

I noted the expression on Marmalady's face.

"Surely a cat as intelligent as *you're* supposed to be, and as well trained, could manage something! You can't have lived with MADAM all these years without acquiring basic education. If you go about it properly you can ask the other cats for help, and in any case they can't refuse - you're Number One. Just begin at the beginning as you see it and go on from there."

Marmalady having made her decision, no matter what trouble it would cause me, lost interest, sat down and began to wash her paws. She settled down in front of the fire and went to sleep.

You can, perhaps, understand why we address Marmalady as M'lady. It's never wise to argue with her - she always has the last word! The way in which she had spoken to me told me in no uncertain manner that she didn't think I was a very clever cat. As I thought over what she had said I decided I would prove to her that I wasn't stupid.

And that's when I acquired problems I never knew existed!

I Don't Know Where To Begin!

But where should I begin? What about the cats I'd never known? I searched my mind for clues, scratched my head in despair, and then I remembered Marmalady's comment: 'We don't need human talk!' She was right, **CATS** don't need human talk!

Of course cats don't need human talk, but I'm not permitted to disclose why we refused the opportunity of learning human language and, instead, decided to develop our own method of communication. And I'm sure you've noticed most humans have this peculiar habit of asking pets a question and then supplying the answer themselves; so there's really no need for us to speak as humans do. However, **WE** understand! **WE** know what humans are saying when they talk to us. Don't we always respond to our doting 'owners' in such a way that they say - "My cat understands every word I say!"

There are times, though, when I have to admit that what humans say puzzles me; it can hardly be called a conversation! For instance ,I overheard a few words spoken by our next door neighbour:

"How's my Boofy Boofy then? Would he like his Foody Woody?"

I've not been able to make up my mind whether she was talking to the baby or the dog!

I don't like dogs! Nasty, smelly, noisy creatures! I'm convinced that owners of dogs only pretend to like cats. I've heard them say "Can't think why anyone wants to keep a cat, except to catch mice! Disgusting creatures, you never know where they've been!"

At least **WE** don't have to be taken for 'walkies'; we can be left for a day provided we have food and shelter; **WE** don't have to be bathed, we wash ourselves!

In my opinion **CATS** make ideal companions even though we are of an independent nature. Having a cat to stroke and pet can be very comforting. (Maybe dog owners feel that way about their dogs!)

There's no doubt that cats are more popular than they used to be. Some humans really like cats, some even love us, but then, there are those who hate us or are frightened of us. I have a lot of sympathy for humans who like cats but can't have one because something about our fur makes them ill. Cats instinctively know when their human friends need close attention and affection.

I'm sorry for those who don't like cats - they don't know what fun there missing

Why, of why couldn't Marmalady have been more helpful and given me some assistance? Begin at the beginning she said. For me the beginning must be when my brother and I joined the group and went to live with SIR, MADAM and ANDREW. We (the cats) are very fond of the FAMILY and if SIR hadn't taken me to KEEPERS I wouldn't be here to tell the tale.

Perhaps I should introduce myself; I'm Hoover. A funny name for a cat? Indeed it is but it's my given human name. Marmalady, you may remember, indicated that I was Number One and that's true. I succeeded to the title when Dad-Cat died in 1984. You see, where there is a group of cats, one of them has to be in charge, otherwise there's neither order nor discipline! When there were ten of us, we looked to Dad-Cat for guidance and now, when carrying out my duties, I always say to myself - 'Now what would Dad-Cat have done?' The title has to be earned and the choice for Number One has to be agreed and approved by the other cats in the group. The tests which have to be taken are quite difficult but I won't bore you with the details. Needless to say that when all was said and done, it was decided I was the only one who could take Dad-Cat's place. Marmalady wasn't too pleased, but then lady-cats aren't allowed to compete.

It may surprise you to know there are more disadvantages than advantages to being Number One. However, some of the privileges are worth having: for instance, I'm allowed to sleep on MADAM's bed (and I usually do), while the others have to make do with boxes in the utility room, except for Marmalady, who has her own basket which she shares with her daughter. I'm always the first to be fed, have first claim to the choice of left-overs and any scraps of fresh meat, but mindful of my duties towards the elderly, I decided that Marmalady should have that privilege; not that she shows any appreciation, but she is very old and holds a position of importance with the FAMILY.

The younger cats are envious of my position and try, occasionally, by making trouble to get their own way. However any stepping out of line is punished immediately. A quick cuff round the ear, a chase round the garden, a few well chosen swear words and they know who's in charge. The respect due to Number One is quickly restored.

I enjoy being Number One!

I'm glad Marmalady isn't looking over my shoulder; if she was, I'd hear her say: "I knew he wouldn't be able to concentrate on what he's been asked to do!"

I have allowed myself to be side-tracked, a human failing I really must try to avoid.

Where was I? Oh yes, the beginning - that's when my brother and I were taken to KEEPERS.

We Join The Cats At Keepers

Hoffman, my twin brother, and I were born in late March 1978 in Balham, London. Some humans refer to Balham as the 'Gateway to the South', though how anyone could call that overcrowded place a gateway, I'll never know! No doubt that's due to some peculiar, human reasoning quite beyond my understanding.

Our mother lived in a small house not far from SIR's office and that was very lucky for us, because if SIR hadn't seen the notice, 'Two long-haired, tabby kittens, eight weeks old, need a good home', we would never have gone to KEEPERS.

It was a long journey in SIR's car and on arrival we were fed and cuddled, provided with a litter tray, and then allowed to settle down for the night in a warm box away from the other cats. Hoff and I didn't know then how lucky we were. Our new 'owners' loved cats (they already had five and there had been seven), and it was the kind of home cats dream about, good food, warm beds, caring friends and lots of affection.

MADAM knew from experience that five big cats, an established group, would be a bit daunting for two small kittens, so several days went by before we were introduced to the other cats. There were many questions, such as 'Where are you from? What do your parents do? Do you appreciate how fortunate you are? Are you house trained? Can you be trusted?' We answered to the best of our ability, overwhelmed and rather frightened.

Rexie Dad-Cat, we were told, was Number One; it was he who would decide admittance to the group. We waited. Would we be accepted? We didn't want to go back to Balham! Dad-Cat came across to where we sat; very gently he licked and scented us and then called Marmalady and her daughters to do the same. You cannot imagine our relief - we had passed inspection and had been accepted into the group.

During the next few days there was some swearing and tail lashing but Dad-Cat had decided we could stay and, as his decisions were law, Hoff and I were only pushed around when we got in the way.

There could never be any doubt as to who was in charge - Rexie Dat-Cat! He was a large, dignified, white cat with ginger markings on his head and tail. A cat with experience and who always, even when confronting danger, appeared cool, calm and collected. I cannot remember a time when Dad-Cat let his feelings get the better of him. If ever a cat walked alone and knew what was what, it was he! But he did have a great affection for the FAMILY and would stand on his hind legs and rub his head against the face of SIR, or MADAM or ANDREW whenever any of THEM bent over him and said, 'Give us a kiss!' He did confide in me that he thought what he did was undignified but it pleased THEM!

Marmalady was then and still is Senior Lady Cat. A superior feline, half Siamese and pure tortoiseshell in colour. She's very aware of her importance to the FAMILY and never, ever lets any of us forget it. When Hoff and I joined the group she was often out hunting and nearly always brought home a rabbit as a special treat. Sometimes when she was hunting she wouldn't come when called and then SIR or MADAM would go looking for her; they worried, thinking that she was lost or hurt because she'd been injured in an accident once before. On those occasions Dad-Cat would call us together and say: "We'd better help in the search to please THEM!", though he knew, and so did the rest of us, that Marmalady would come when she felt like it!

Over the fields, through the woods or down the lane,

SIR or MADAM walking in front, six cats in line behind as if they were chained together. THEY searched and called until Marmalady decided to show herself, safe and sound, and we could most thankfully turn for home. A very independent cat is Marmalady!

What passers-by or people in cars thought of our expedition - my imagination doesn't stretch that far!

Marmalita, Marmasetta and Penny-Gelly were Marmalady's daughters. Marmalita and Marmasetta had their names shortened to Lita and Setta - they were both tortoiseshell and white. While Lita was a great talker, (and still is for that matter), Setta was quiet and much given to disappearing to some secret place on her own. Penny-Gelly, or more correctly, Penelope-Pengelly, was ginger and white and very thin. I was sorry for her because she always seemed frightened and though, she was a loving cat, she often missed out on her share of cuddles. She had the bad habit of hanging on with her claws when picked up and it used to annoy MADAM, especially if she was wearing something nice. ANDREW was Penny-Gelly's favourite and she would sit patiently by his side, waiting to be noticed. Sadly she died soon after we came to Devon. The FAMILY buried Penny-Gelly in the orchard where she liked to sit when it was warm and the sun was shining.

Charles Marmaduke and Felicity Farnes-Barnes were Marmalady's other children, but Hoff and I never knew them; MADAM mentions their names now and then, but that's all. I've heard the names Timothy-Tuddle and Humphrey-Bumphrey; I have the idea that they weren't made full members of the group and could be some of the cats Marmalady refers to as 'Intruders'!

I must remember to ask about them.

KEEPERS had been a gamekeeper's cottage. It didn't look old from the outside, because there had been some additions. Inside there were old oak beams in the low ceilings and thick walls to keep out the cold. In one room, which the FAMILY called the Snug, there was a big open fireplace; in the winter log fires were very popular. Hoff would curl up on MADAM's lap, I on ANDREW's, Dad-Cat and Marmalady on the seats inside the fireplace and the others on the rug in front of the fire. (That fireplace was to play a big part in the life of one my brothers when SIR brought him from Balham to join the group.)

I miss KEEPERS, its garden, woodland and surrounding fields - a paradise for cats. The only other animals in sight, sheep and cows from nearby farms; the nearest house, a half a mile away. What a contrast WITH Balham!

The house we live in now is very different and has much more room. According to MADAM it has a beautiful view but a view doesn't mean much to cats! We cats, of course, weren't given a choice. We had to go where the FAMILY decided to go!

Keepers

Settling In!

In no time at all it seemed that Hoff and I had always lived at KEEPERS and our memories of Balham began to fade. We had to be careful not to annoy the older cats or we had sharp reminders from Dad-Cat but, perhaps because we were kittens, we were surrounded by affection, especially from MADAM and ANDREW. We only saw SIR at the weekends but we held him in great respect.

I suppose it was unfair that so much was made of us; we didn't realise it at the time and made the most of the situation. If truth be told Hoff and I were not always the sweet, little kittens MADAM thought we were and Marmalady could often be heard saying, "Dad-Cat should not have allowed those kittens into the group, they're nothing but trouble!"

Hoff and I were often given small pieces of roast meat or chicken which, by rights, should have gone to the older cats, and on one occasion we were given some pork sausage. I became very fond of pork sausage.

Usually, on a Saturday, the FAMILY would have their meals on trays and watch television in the Snug; we cats would wait for tit-bits. I can remember there was this bit of sausage on MADAM's plate - I hooked it off and ate it up quickly; it was delicious! I didn't think of what could happen and looked for more and then realised I was being watched. I tried to look innocent, (stealing food even now, is punished by a smack), but luckily for me there was lots of laughter and I was just given a scolding, much to the annoyance of the other cats.

Lita was most put out and complained to Dad-Cat but he said he was sure I'd learn from my mistakes.

He was right, I have. It's a useful trick which amuses the FAMILY. Nowadays if they're eating sausages I'm encouraged to hook pieces off their trays! However, I don't think it's at all kind to call me a 'Sausage Stealer' and more recently a 'Pork Pie Pastry Pincher', because I've taken a liking to that as well!

Side-tracked again! I really must watch what I'm doing.

But there were times when Hoff and I behaved badly and got into trouble; being young and playful we did things which upset the older cats and Dad-Cat would be asked to deal with us. If he said 'Hoover, Hoffman, BEHAVE!', once, he said it a thousand times!

Hoff, because he thought he was extra special, being, as he said, MADAM's cat, was often out of order and forgetting he was a junior cat, began to think he could do wrong. Sometimes he was so unbearable that I had to agree with Dad-Cat that his behaviour was unacceptable.

Hoff, as a kitten had the makings of a handsome cat, and he did become one, with long, silky fur with perfect tabby markings, but he was not, what you'd call, 'very bright'!

So, despite repeated warnings from Dad-Cat as to how he should behave, Hoff continued to overstep the mark. He would creep up on Lita when she was peacefully sunning herself in the garden; pounce on Penny-Gelly when she was sleeping, so that she'd jump out of her box in a fright; he'd steal Setta's food when she wasn't looking; and persisted in playing with Marmalady's tail - much to her annoyance. She'd give him a swipe around his ears, but it had little effect.

Something Horrible Happened!

The day finally came when Dad-Cat lost all patience, took Hoff to one side, dealt with him severely and said: "Enough is enough! Marmalady finds you a nuisance and so do I! If you don't mind your paws and behave better something horrible will happen to you!"

It was a strong threat but Dad-Cat's warning made no difference - Hoff continued to behave badly, quite convinced that MADAM would protect him and rescue him from any danger. A few weeks later I learned that Dad-Cat's threat wasn't a bluff.

It was a very unpleasant surprise.

One morning Hoff and I were bundled into a basket, carried out to MADAM's car and taken into the village. The car stopped outside a large building and we were taken into a room smelling of DOG and strange cats. I was scared and so was Hoff, but as usual full of bravado, he declared there was nothing to worry about, 'after all wasn't MADAM there to take care of us?'

A few minutes later MADAM picked up the basket and I heard someone say, "You can go in now."

We entered another room and MADAM put the basket on a table, undid the catch and lifted me out saying, "Good morning, Mr B, I think they're old enough now, don't you? They're nearly six months old."

I was up-ended, very rudely, and the man agreed, I was old enough! Old enough for what I thought? The same thing was done to Hoff but he had to disgrace himself, much to MADAM's embarrassment.

"Yes," said the man. "He's about right as well. Leave them with us. Ring up about three to find out when you can collect them."

I began miaowing plaintively, "Don't leave me!" trying hard to attract MADAM's attention. That's when I regretted that humans didn't understand cat language. And I couldn't speak theirs.

Hoff and I were taken away to a big cage and a little while later a young man came and gave us injections. I thought it was for cat-flu but as I started to feel sleepy, Dad-Cat's words came to mind, *"Something horrible will happen if ... "* and I thought, 'This is the threatened punishment!' - and then, nothing.

When I came to my legs and paws wouldn't hold me up and each time I tried to stand I fell over. Something horrible *had* happened. Why had MADAM agreed that it should happen? I felt dreadful but Hoff seemed worse. He was moaning and groaning as though in great pain, as if his last hour had come. I examined him carefully but as I couldn't find any cuts, bruises or scratches, I came to the conclusion that he wasn't that bad, just looking for sympathy. In fact I became angry and told him to stop performing. I made it clear that if he'd behaved and been obedient, we wouldn't have ended up in a nasty situation.

I couldn't believe that MADAM, whom we trusted, had given permission for Hoff and me to be punished. What had I done to deserve such treatment? It seemed to me that in future there could only be one possible course of action - I would try to be a GOOD, OBEDIENT CAT, listen to my elders and take note when I felt tingling in my paws, a sure sign of trouble. I advised Hoff to do the same but he didn't take any notice, not then or afterwards. He just howled, making so much noise that the young man who'd given us injections came to have a look at him. Of course there was nothing the matter, Hoff just wanted to be the centre of attention as usual. But I waited quietly, wondering if I'd ever see KEEPERS again.

It was some hours later when I heard MADAM's voice

and began to feel a little happier. She made a great fuss of Hoff as she put him in the basket to be taken home. Hoff lapped it up, miaowing loudly and behaving as though he was being rescued from the jaws of death. I put on an air of disdain and boredom, and looked the other way; I wasn't going to let HER know how worried I had been. MADAM made an even greater fuss of me. She rubbed my ears, tickled my chin and she gave me a hug, but I wasn't having any of that, *I ignored her.* I wouldn't give her the satisfaction of knowing I cared.

I think she got my message and gave up trying to make me purr, for as MADAM put me in the basket, I heard her say, "Oh he'll come round when he wants some food. By tomorrow, Hoover will have forgotten all about it." I had a quiet smirk to myself - little did she know. Cats have long memories, but often choose to have short ones!

When we got back to KEEPERS, Hoff and I were greeted by the other cats who were waiting to find out what had happened. Dad-Cat looked smug and gave Hoff a knowing look as he listened to our story.

"Well, Hoffman," Dad-Cat was very formal, "What did I tell you? Perhaps in future, when you're given good advice, you'll pay attention and do as you're told."

Hoff looked suitably ashamed and Dad-Cat walked away, pleased that his words had made some impression. I was intrigued with Dad-Cat's reaction to our story and decided that, when I had an opportunity, I'd ask him why he though something horrible would happen if Hoff didn't behave. (Though on reflection I can't think why I was punished as well, I was never as bad as Hoff!)

Dad-Cat's Punishment

Later that evening I had the chance of talking to Dad-Cat.

"Dad-Cat, what made you say that something horrible would happen to Hoff if he didn't behave?"

"Well, young Hoover, you could call it intuition. You see I'm fairly certain that I was punished in a similar way. But not, I think, for bad behaviour."

"What were you punished for, then?" I prompted.

"Perhaps there's time to tell you before bed. Listen carefully and take note. Humans do things we don't always understand. Some can't be trusted, others are unpredictable." Dad-Cat scratched himself thoughtfully.

"My mother was a Turkish Van. As you can see, I have all the markings but unfortunately I didn't develop long-haired fur, so the humans who bought me, hoping they'd be able to show me as a champion, were disappointed. They took me into the country and left me there. I was about a year old at the time and didn't know how to fend for myself. The first few months were very hard and if it hadn't been for my determination to survive, I would have died of starvation."

"But why were you punished?" I interrupted.

Dad-Cat ignored me and went on, "Still I survived, more by luck than judgement. I learnt to catch rabbits and there were plenty of mice in the barns around here. Then there were times when some humans took pity on me and left out scraps and a saucer of milk." Dad-Cat seemed lost in his memories and I was becoming impatient; I wondered if he'd ever get to the end!

Dad-Cat continued. "The other cats who lived around here were no match for me and had to accept me as their leader.

But one day while I was searching for food, a farmer took a pot shot at me. He thought it was me who dug up his garden, not realising that it was the rabbits I hunted who did the damage."

"Dad-Cat, I don't wish to be rude, but what has that got to do with punishment?" and I thought to myself, *I wish he'd get on!*

He gave me a gentle cuff round the ear. "I'm coming to that. I was laid up for several weeks; the lead shot is still in my right leg and shoulder. Wounds don't heal quickly in the winter and when I was back on my feet, much to my surprise, I'd become the local hero with the lady cats who followed me everywhere; I had nothing but problems with the other Toms."

"DAD-CAT ... "

He held up his paw to stop me saying any more. "And then I met Marmalady! I'll never forget that moment. It was Christmas time; the FAMILY had only been at KEEPERS a few months. I was just wandering around when I saw her; she was sitting on the doorstep, sniffing the air and enjoying some winter sunshine. I stopped for a brief miaow - and that was that! I've been devoted to her ever since. She had such an innocent expression; I knew at once no Tom had ever made advances to her. With my experience it didn't take long to have her purring away as if she'd known me all her life," Dad-Cat paused. "I suppose I did take advantage of her. When she realised what had happened, she was not at all pleased. As you know, Marmalady still warns me off if I get too close!"

Dad-Cat was being so long-winded, I despaired of ever hearing why he'd been punished. I was getting tired and yawned.

"Don't yawn like that, Hoover, it's bad-mannered."

I apologised at once and asked him to continue.

"The following March Marmalady had five kittens. I was delighted and came to see them every day and I think I would've come even if I'd known what was going to happen. MADAM encouraged me with food and milk, a bed was made available in a garden shed. The food got closer and closer to the cottage until one morning it was in the kitchen! I was a bit surprised but I'd learnt to trust MADAM, she was always kind. I ate my food, inspected the kittens, was about to go, when before you could say 'Wash your paws', I was in a basket and I'm very sure I made the same journey as you, went to the same place and, *I'm very sure,* I had the self same experience!"

I looked at Dad-Cat. "Do you mean ... ?" I queried.

Dad-Cat nodded his head in answer to my unspoken question.

"Do you remember anything of what happened?"

"No. I think I was punished for taking advantage of Marmalady. I've no idea what Mr. B. did to me but I do know from that day to this, I've never fancied another lady-cat. I've remained faithful to Marmalady and, you know, there's lots to be said for regular meals and a warm bed at night."

Dad-Cat got up, stretched, yawned and jumped up into his favourite chair. He turned round once or twice, settled comfortably, curled his tail over his nose and went to sleep.

I thought over what he'd said. Dad-Cat was so very wise. Cats would never quite understand the whys and wherefores of humans. As he'd said THEY WERE UNPREDICTABLE AND NOT ALWAYS TO BE TRUSTED!

Rexie Dad - Cat

Burglars!

Not long after my visit to Mr. B, whom I now know was a vet and probably still is one, we all suffered a very frightening experience. KEEPERS WAS BURGLED!

MADAM was a teacher and travelled to Solihull every day. ANDREW went with her because he attended school nearby, so they were away all day and SIR worked in London during the week. No one knew until later that the daily comings and goings were being watched and the times noted when the cottage was empty, except for us cats.

That particular morning we were all asleep in our boxes in the kitchen when Marmalady alerted us to the presence of strangers. We heard voices, not ones we recognised. We sat up, feeling very anxious, usually it was so quiet. Few people called in the day and we knew the milkman and postman well; it was past their time.

Suddenly the glass in the kitchen window shattered, glass was scattered all over the floor as a hand came through to undo the latch. Needless to say that as a man climbed in the window we all made a dash for the cat-flap! We were terrified, we panicked; Dad-Cat got stuck with Marmalady, while the rest of us pushed and shoved as hard as we could from behind. A fight broke out between Lita and Penny-Gelly. (Even now I am overcome with fright.) I didn't know what to do, Instinct told me to run but instead I retreated under the tea trolley, hoping I wouldn't be seen. The first man was joined by a second; they stood and laughed as Penny-Gelly and Setta still struggled to get through the cat-flap. I watched in horror as Setta was helped on her way with a kick in the rear. (I have often thought since then that it was the kick which caused Setta's illness, which gave her so much pain in the months that followed.)

I crouched low, knowing only too well what the other cats would be thinking, 'Had these men come to kill us? Did they want our fur?' So many of our friends had disappeared recently without trace.

The men ignored me, so I kept as far out of sight as possible and breathed a sigh of relief, though my heart was beating nineteen to the dozen. I watched the men open the fridge door and help themselves to food and drink. Perhaps they were friends of the FAMILY after all and then ...

"We can't hang about down here all day. We'd better see what we can find that's worth taking," said the younger of the two men.

"Right then, you go upstairs and I'll have a look round down here. At least we shouldn't be disturbed now the cats have gone, not that they posed much of a threat!" said the older man and they both laughed.

I took a peep from my hiding place; thank goodness they didn't want cat fur, but there were nice things in the Snug and upstairs. The men looked very rough; they were wearing dirty, dark blue overalls. One of them opened the door into the Snug and they were gone. As soon as the door shut I was through the cat-flap in a flash, and running for cover in the woodland where I knew I'd be safe.

Dad-Cat and Marmalady were watching from the trees nearby and Hoff, who now came to join me, began asking silly questions such as "Did I know what was happening, and what were the men doing in the cottage?" Typical of Hoff of course; I told him to save his breath and keep running until we reached our hiding place in the woods. We stayed for hours, much too frightened to move; it was dark when we heard MADAM calling. Hoff rushed off at once, but I was beginning to feel the after-effects of fright and could only walk slowly towards KEEPERS.

I felt quite ill and after a while gave up trying to reach the cottage and just curled up where I was, hoping that MADAM or ANDREW would come looking for me. I heard them calling but I didn't have the strength to respond. Luckily there was no rain that night; otherwise I don't think I would have survived.

It was not until the next day that I learned that MADAM thought I'd been killed and hidden under a pile of clothing in her bedroom. You must know that when there's been a burglary, nothing must be touched until the police have searched for clues and checked for fingerprints, so it was late in the evening when the FAMILY knew that possibly I was alive but missing. I can imagine MADAM's sigh of relief when the clothing was removed and NO DEAD CAT!

It became very cold towards morning and I knew I had to make one last effort to reach the cottage. I began walking, pausing now and then to rest and get my breath, each pause longer than the one before. I just hoped I'd get to a spot where I could see the cottage and be seen. And then, there it was - I was home! I couldn't have gone any further, I was too tired. I waited and I suppose I fell asleep, for suddenly I realised that Dad-Cat was licking my face, Hoff was making a lot of noise, and the other cats were running to and fro, pleased to see me alive!

But to me, best of all was seeing SIR, MADAM and ANDREW.

Madam bent over me: "Oh Hoover, we all thought you were dead and we were so unhappy to think we'd never see you again. Thank goodness you're safe." MADAM made sure I wasn't injured in any way and ANDREW picked me up, very carefully, and carried me home to KEEPERS.

However, one thing did mar my home-coming. MADAM insisted that I should be taken to see Mr. B and, (as if I hadn't suffered enough), I had to have injections because it took some time for me to recover from fright and exposure.

Hoff wasn't in the least bit sympathetic. Much to his annoyance he wasn't getting all the attention he thought was his right. I did tell him he shouldn't have been so eager to run home and then he could've had some injections as well! He didn't speak to me for several days. But one good thing came of the upset - from that day I was given permission to sleep on ANDREW's bed. I was, as he said, HIS CAT.

None of the things stolen from the cottage were recovered, but a few months later the Police informed SIR and MADAM that the men who'd broken into KEEPERS had been arrested and sent to prison.

Marmasetta

It was many months before we all felt it was safe to stay indoors during the day. However, none of us realised that Setta had been hurt but within several weeks of the burglary Setta began to fail.

You will remember that I said a well-aimed kick had helped her through the cat-flap. We cats had no doubts, that was the time when the damage was done. At first Setta couldn't run properly and then her judgement when jumping into her box, or onto the seats by the fire seemed to let her down. Some days were better than others. It soon became clear that something was wrong with her back legs and that her back lacked the suppleness a cat needs when it jumps and climbs. Setta didn't complain but she was often in pain. Even Hoff, who was a most selfish cat, could see that she wasn't well and gave up his place on MADAM's lap so that Setta could have cuddles.

MADAM took Setta to Mr. B. and different treatments were tried but there was no improvement; finally she was left with Mr. B. for a thorough examination. Later when MADAM went to fetch her, Dad-Cat told us to be prepared for the worst; we sat around waiting for them to return; it wasn't a happy home-coming. We thought Setta was sleeping peacefully in the basket but MADAM looked very sad.

Dad-Cat called us together in the kitchen.

"Just as well it's the weekend and SIR's home. He'll know what to say and do. Be very quiet, all of you, and listen."

We heard SIR talking to MADAM. "What was the trouble?"

"Setta had spondulitis. When Mr. B. gave her a full examination, he found that her spine had already begun to set

26

and eventually she wouldn't have been able to move at all."

"Wasn't there anything he could do?"

"Mr. B. did say that with treatment he could ease her pain and keep her alive for perhaps another year, but in the end ... " MADAM continued, "I couldn't sentence Setta to months of confinement in the house. She's always liked to be out in the woods, on her own, independent and free. Well, ... now she's permanently free. We'll put her in the garden next to Charles and Felicity." MADAM turned away and went upstairs. I nudged Hoff, and we followed; we found her looking out of the window in her bedroom.

You will, no doubt, have come to the conclusion that I didn't have a high opinion of my brother Hoff, but just for once he thought of someone other than himself. He begged MADAM to pick him up and showed his affection by rubbing his head against her hand while I sat at her feet and rubbed my face against her legs; we both purred as loudly as we could and hoped she knew what we were trying to express. We wanted her to know how much we cared.

There are occasions when pets can be more understanding than the humans who are closest to you. We can't give you words, but aren't our warmth and silent sympathy, sometimes, more acceptable?

Later that day Setta was buried in the garden next to her brother and sister and when SIR, MADAM and ANDREW had gone back to the cottage, we paid our respects and made our farewells. Dad-Cat and Marmalady were so sad; of their five kittens only Lita and Penny-Gelly were still with them.

I've never ceased to be thankful that I stayed out of sight; I don't like to think of what those men might have done to me.

Marmalady's Story

I'd been wondering what to tell you next and was putting my thoughts in order, (thinking of the arrival in 1980 of one of my brothers and a sister), when I realised that Marmalady was paying me more attention than usual.

"What are you doing, Hoover? You've been very busy these last few days and you've not been attending to your duties as No.1 should."

That was true, but I didn't need Marmalady to remind me.

"I'm sorry if I seem neglectful, M'lady, but I've been following up your suggestion that I should set down what I know about KEEPERS cats and I was thinking about the arrival of my brothers and sister."

Marmalady's expression seemed to indicate that for once I had her approval! "I'm glad you took my advice. If there's anything I can do to help, let me know."

I couldn't believe my ears! Marmalady offering help! Usually she's one of the most stand-offish cats you could ever hope to meet and only deigns to pass the time of day if she thinks there's nothing better to do!

As she seemed in a reasonably friendly mood, the chance to ask questions couldn't be missed. But would she tell me what I wanted to know? Some of the questions I wanted to ask were personal; Marmalady is 18 years old, we all treat her with great respect and make sure we don't offend her.

"I would appreciate some help, M'lady. After all, you've been with the FAMILY the longest. How was it that KEEPERS became your home? Were you a kitten?"

I waited. Did she really mean to help?

Marmalady found a suitably sunny spot in the window,

settled herself comfortably and began to wash her face as though she was considering what to say.

"I'm sure you're aware that I'm very important to the FAMILY and while I'm not No. 1 - being a lady-cat I couldn't aspire to that position - none the less I have great influence. I joined the FAMILY in December 1971. They'd only been at KEEPERS a short time, having recently returned from Belgium and, fortunately for me, were looking for a cat. I've learnt from conversations that the FAMILY lost a well-loved cat, called Peter Podge, while they were living in Antwerp. Sometimes MADAM mentions his name; he obviously meant a great deal to them. I believe he had a brother called Simon but they don't say much about him." Marmalady paused as though lost in thought. "KEEPERS was a nice place for cats; the FAMILY didn't spoil it. They made the garden more orderly, cut down dead trees in the woodland and, as you know, added a new kitchen and turned the old one into a dining room. There were a few changes to the outside but it was always KEEPERS. And thinking about it, I liked the cottage more than this place."

"But how did you come to join the FAMILY?" I asked her again. "Were you a kitten?" It was dangerous ground; I knew from Dad-Cat that she hadn't been a kitten, but I couldn't remember her ever talking about her first home.

"Perhaps you could say I was a lucky cat. Luck has certainly played a big part in my life." Marmalady looked out of the window and I wondered if she would go on; she sighed. "I was born in Birmingham. My mother was a Siamese seal-point of champion class; her breeding was impeccable but she was not very clever, somewhat foolish and easily influenced. She fell for and was led astray by a big, black Tom. I and my two brothers were the result."

I almost said, "But didn't Dad-Cat lead you astray?" and remembered just in time to hold my tongue. A set-to with

Marmalady was not what I was looking for!

"When I was about 2 years old my first 'owner' gave me away to some friends and I went to live in Selly Oak. In those days I was known as 'Soo-Long' and, at first, everything was fine. I had a good home, plenty to eat and kind 'owners'; but then the grandchildren came to stay. They began to torment me, pulling my tail, snatching my food away just as I had settled, shutting me in a cupboard and sometimes chasing me round and round the garden. I didn't know what to do. I couldn't tell the grandparents, you know why, but of course when they were looking, those two little boys loved pussy-cats! I was so unhappy and scared that finally, after one very bad day I don't like to think about, I ran away!

I could see how the memories of those days distressed Marmalady so I gently licked her face in sympathy.

"I didn't look where I was going and the next thing I knew I was lying in the road - I'd been hit by a car."

"Didn't anyone come to help you?" I asked.

Marmalady shook her head. "I shall never forget how frightened I was. My back right leg was broken and there was blood all over my fur. I lay there hoping that I wouldn't be hit again. To this day the sound and smell of traffic terrifies me." She licked her paws in some agitation. "I'd almost given up hope of being rescued when luck came into my life for the first time. Someone picked me up very gently and carried me to the Animal Hospital which Mr. B. had in Selly-Oak, A young lady washed the blood from my fur and Mr. B. set my leg in plaster."

"Was it MADAM who found you?"

Marmalady waved her tail from side to side, she was very upset. "No; and no one asked for me! I was well cared for and once my broken leg healed, I was sent to Alvechurch and that's when luck entered my life for the second time."

At that moment MADAM called us for our evening meal

and Marmalady seemed pleased that she could stop. Past memories were proving too much for her; she was finding it difficult to maintain her dignified approach to life.

"I'll finish my story later, Hoover. I shall rest for a while after we've eaten."

What could I say, except, "Thank you!"! I had to hope that her present willingness to talk would last.

Marmalady Continues Her Story

Later that evening, as we were peacefully dozing by the fire, Marmalady came to sit beside me; she was not the 'don't come near me cat' I was used to.

"Would you like to put off telling me the rest of your story until tomorrow, M'lady?"

"No, Hoover. Tomorrow won't make it any better. I haven't enjoyed thinking about a past I'd rather forget. You needn't worry, but - where was I?"

"You were talking about the time when luck entered your life for the second time."

"Oh, yes. When I was fully recovered from my injuries I was allowed the run of the hospital. Everyone made a fuss of me but it wasn't the same as having a real home. Then one day as I was passing by Mr. B.'s room I saw MADAM enter, carrying two kittens. Something prompted me to stop and watch. I heard Mr. B. say that the kittens were not healthy and should be returned to the RSPCA; I felt a pricking in my paws and knew that was the moment I'd been waiting for. I ran into the room, jumped up on the window sill and did everything I could to attract attention. MADAM noticed me and asked Mr. B. about me saying, wasn't I a beautiful cat. Mr. B. said I needed a home so I went over to MADAM and begged to be picked up. I knew she liked me and I sensed she was a cat-person as soon as she touched me. The next few minutes seemed like hours while I waited for her decision. I purred with delight when I heard her say, 'We'll give it a try, if it doesn't work, we'll have to bring her back.'"

"So that's how you found yourself a home and a FAMILY."

"Indeed it was. Every day I try to tell MADAM how

grateful I am that she came to Mr. B.'s that day." Marmalady stopped.

I wasn't sure whether she had finished her story or not so I thought I'd ask her how she'd got her present name.

"MADAM took me home. I was given a bowl of food and a basket which Lita now shares. Both SIR and ANDREW made much of me and it was then that I was given a new name. ANDREW said the colour of my fur reminded him of something humans call 'Marmalade' and so I was named."

I was quite puzzled. "But you're called Marmalady?"

"That's right. When ANDREW had his school holidays they weren't always the same as MADAM's. A friend, called UNCLE ERIC used to come and stay, and as he insisted on calling me a HE, the FAMILY thought that by adding a 'Y' he'd get the idea I was a SHE, and there you are."

Marmalady got up, stretched and was about to go away when I remembered she said that her name had been Soo-Long.

"Just a couple more questions, M'lady, if it's not too much trouble."

I expected to be ignored for she appeared to have lost interest. "What is it now?" she replied impatiently.

"You did mention earlier, M'lady, that at one time you were called Soo-Long."

Marmalady sat down. "I don't know why I told you that, except that thinking about what happened before I went to KEEPERS reminded me of a strange coincidence. I had been with the FAMILY two or three years when MADAM brought home a visitor. I was sitting on the driveway and I couldn't believe my eyes, when out of MADAM's car, who should step but my mother's 'owner'!"

"What did you do? Run away?"

"No. Unfortunately she recognised me and was quite angry. She demanded to know what was MADAM doing with

33

a cat she'd given to friends in Selly-Oak. She almost accused MADAM of stealing me but MADAM replied quickly, saying there couldn't be any connection because I'd come from the local cats' home! The answer must have convinced my mother's 'owner' and I was left in peace. Any other questions?"

Did I dare ask the last question I had in mind?

"How did Dad-Cat join the FAMILY and become No. 1?"

"That's something I do not care to discuss and if you want any more information, I suggest you talk to Lita, she's always ready for a chat!"

Marmalady got up, stretched and moved across to the place she normally occupied immediately in front of the fire. Littlechap and Littlesusie made way for her as she settled herself in the best and warmest place, checking that none of the other cats were too close for her comfort.

I thought to myself: "I knew you wouldn't answer that question about Dad-Cat, M'lady, and I doubt if you'll give me the chance to ask any more! Marmalady - a most superior cat! How could MADAM have said you'd come from the local cats' home?"

The woodland, our hiding - place!

Six Become Eight

SIR is, without a doubt, a soft touch when it comes to cats and I'm of the opinion he thought MADAM needed a replacement or replacements for Setta. He'd seen another notice: "Two kittens need loving home". Perhaps you can guess the whereabouts of that notice? You're right - on the gate of the house where Hoff and I had been born.

MADAM had said very emphatically six cats were more than enough but, one Friday evening, SIR returned from London with a cardboard box in the boot of his car. It was May 1980.

SIR brought the box into the Snug and put it down on the carpet, unopened. I didn't know at the time that inside were a brother and sister. (We had the same mother but looking at Littlechap, I think maybe, although he is short-haired, we even had the same father.) It so happened that we were all in, waiting for our evening meal and we were overcome with curiosity, wondering what could be inside the box. To anyone who was watching, it must have been a funny sight: six cats approaching a cardboard box, very cautiously, inch by inch. Then, when the lid flew off, scattering to hiding places round the room as a small bundle of fur erupted from the box, a spitting, clawing kitten, ears flat and tail erect. A very small kitten, ready to do battle whatever the odds!

I peered from my hiding place to see one little black head peeping over the top of the box while the fighting bundle of tabby fur was disappearing rapidly beneath the fire grate. That kitten didn't know how lucky he was. *Being Friday the fire hadn't been lit!* SIR grabbed the kitten by his tail and pulled him out, covered with wood-ash but still fighting.

MADAM gathered him up with one hand, picked up the box which still had the little black kitten inside and took them

36

both away to give them food and put them in a quiet place to sleep. When MADAM returned, I knew from the expression on her face, she was worried.

The very next day when the kittens were brought into the Snug for the second time, tabby kitten made for the fireplace again; but where the previous evening there had been cold ashes, now there was a RED-HOT LOG FIRE! I watched in horror as he disappeared under the grate. The smell of singed fur filled the room as once again SIR rescued this most belligerent of kittens.

"Poor Littlechap," said SIR and the name stuck. Indeed he was a sorry sight; the fur on his back blackened and burnt, his front paws blistered from the heat. SIR gave him to MADAM who tried to calm him down but with little success. Littlechap spat, swore, scratched and howled with anger and fright, so he was taken away to a warm covered box.

MADAM was most concerned. "That's the first time in many a year that I've had to put on gloves to handle a kitten. We're going to have problems with that one."

The little black kitten who was Littlechap's sister and mine, was named Littlesusie; she settled quickly and, though rather quiet and shy, she was soon well loved by the FAMILY and firm friends with Lita and Penny-Gelly. She was accepted by the group but as for Littlechap, as the days went by and there was no change in his behaviour, since he was still wild and difficult, his chances of acceptance became less and less.

One morning I heard MADAM say, "I hope he's not a rogue cat. If he is there's nothing I can do but if he's just frightened, maybe I can 'psych' him. If not, he has to go."

Dad-Cat shook his head. "I wish her luck," he whispered. "Few humans can do that successfully!"

The situation with Littlechap grew steadily worse. Even Dad-Cat with his wealth of experience could do nothing with him.

"It's down to MADAM now. I can't get through to him. He's frightened out of his wits, so much so that he doesn't trust his own kind - and humans, not at all. You must leave him alone."

We took notice of what Dad-Cat had said and in any case none of us could approach within a paw's length before Littlechap began to spit and swear and take up a defensive position. Littlesusie was the only one who could get close; he slept with her at night but even she couldn't make him see sense.

The day of reckoning came. "Enough is enough! Either Littlechap is tamed or he goes back to Balham," said MADAM.

Later that evening, watching Littlechap cowering under a chair, I thought it would be such a shame if my brother was sent away in disgrace. Despite Dad-Cat's warning I decided to make one last attempt to make him listen. I managed to hold him down for about five seconds, getting my nose badly scratched for my pains.

"Littlechap, no one wants to hurt you. You'd like it here if you gave it a chance. The FAMILY love cats but they'll send you back to Balham if you don't calm down."

He didn't listen to what I'd said and ran away to hide. Hoff licked my scratches sympathetically but he couldn't understand why I was wasting my time on Littlechap. Hoff I knew was only thinking of himself, he didn't like upsets but as he said: "He's getting more than his fair share of attention and making our lives uncomfortable. The best place for him is Balham!" There was a lot of truth in what he said.

Psyching Littlechap

The following day I watched MADAM put on thick gloves; she was going to 'psych' Littlechap! It was his last chance and I didn't like to think that she might fail.

Psyching a cat is very difficult. Whoever tries must have a great affection for cats, understand their ways, know how they communicate, be able to control them and yet have respect for their independence. Not only that, the cat will struggle, bite and scratch. Cat scratches can be very painful and should receive proper treatment. A cat never surrenders willingly; back-off, YES, that's common sense; but surrender, NO! Only when the opponent is the stronger will the cat give in.

I sat well out of sight as did the other cats, pretending that we weren't interested as MADAM picked up Littlechap, gently but firmly. He struggled, he squealed, he spat, he swore and tried all manner of tricks to get free. But slowly and surely he was forced to give in. MADAM turned him on to his back, putting him in the 'surrender' position; he was held securely on her lap, his head held between her hands. Littlechap squirmed but he couldn't break free and was forced to look up at MADAM. She began to massage each side of his eyes, his ears and under his chin; she began to talk to him in a quiet voice.

"Littlechap, stop fighting, calm down and do as I tell you. Be a good kitten and go to sleep." MADAM repeated the words over and over again; and then - softly at first - I heard Littlechap purring. It was the first time he'd ever purred!

The purring grew louder as he relaxed and went to sleep. MADAM allowed him to curl up on her lap; she cuddled him close but it was some time before she took off the gloves and stroked him.

Success! I realised that I was holding my breath and let it

out with a sigh of relief. Looking round the room it was obvious that all of us cats were as mesmerised as Littlechap. Of course he had to be 'psyched' several times but from that day, Littlechap was a changed cat. He stopped fighting and swearing, he was able to control his behaviour and Dad-Cat allowed him to join the group!

Today he's one of the happiest, most cheerful, bounciest of cats you're ever likely to meet. He's devoted to MADAM and follows her about in the house and in the garden. When she showers or baths he has to sit on the bathroom stool; if she's out, he must sit in her chair. And it's quite funny if he can't find her - he's developed a special call to attract her attention: "Ik, Ik Youawl. Ik, Ik, Youawl!" meaning, 'where are you?' A most peculiar noise. But would you believe me when I say MADAM responds in kind until Littlechap finds her. What the neighbours must think of a human using cat language - well, I'll leave that to you.

Incidentally, I wouldn't advise 'psyching' a cat. You really need to know what you're doing!

Littlechap at rest.

41

Cats Were Never Slaves!

I have the idea that SIR would say "I've been too clever for my own good!" He could be right but I know that while I say SIR and MADAM are our 'owners', they talk to us and treat us as equals, not pets, but companions. They respect our independence. No doubt I'm asking for my tail to be pulled but it was Marmalady who made me think most carefully about the relationship between humans and cats.

I'd been considering what to say about our methods of communication and how I should explain them, when unthinkingly, because I was watching Littlechap do a 'roll-over' for MADAM, I said "MADAM's slave, as usual!" What I didn't know was that Marmalady was right behind me and gave me such a cuff round the ears that I couldn't hear properly for at least five minutes!

I turned on Marmalady, paw at the ready. Her tail was waving wildly from side to side, she was very angry!

"To this day, Hoover, I'll never know why we made you No. 1. As SIR says 'You're as thick as six planks!' SLAVE indeed!"

I was astonished. *I*, No. 1, attacked by a mere female! I tried to look dignified, grateful that all the other cats were in the garden.

Marmalady continued her attack. "It's about time you did some research into CAT MEMORY. You think you're a well-educated cat, but in my opinion you're as stupid as your brother was!"

"M'lady, I didn't mean Littlechap was a slave. I meant..."

"You don't know what you did mean. More's the pity." Marmalady walked away, every movement expressing her anger and disgust.

She was right (not that I'd admit it to her). What did I mean? 'Cat Memory' is passed from generation to generation; a way of life, a reference book, history. I thought over Marmalady's words. *How could* I have called a cat 'a slave'? Here was I trying to think of a simple way to explain cat communication and I'd forgotten the most important part of our history!

CATS HAVE NEVER BEEN SLAVES! If anything 'the claw's on the other paw'!

Cat history goes back beyond the arrival of Man and though we have lived beside you for the last 4,000 years, *NEVER, EVER* have we been your slaves. Friends and companions, yes; but slaves, NO! I hear you, I hear you! Friends don't expect to be cared for on a regular basis. There had to be some changes when you invited us into your homes. In the wild we could look after ourselves but when we entered *at your invitation*, we had to adopt a more civilised approach to life!

May I remind you that the Egyptians worshipped us and had a cat goddess, Bashtet; and when the FAMILY cat died, members of the FAMILY went into mourning, shaved off their hair and bewailed the cat's departure! It was forbidden by Egyptian law to kill a cat, just in case the Cat God took revenge. (*What a pity that law doesn't apply nowadays!*) But Egypt was overrun, our lives changed and since then we've been persecuted, burnt, hanged, tortured and treated with suspicion. For instance, did you know that at the coronation of Queen Elizabeth I, some cats were put in a wicker basket called a 'pope' and burned alive?

So much for human kindness in the past. However, not everyone condemned the cat! It may surprise you to know that in France we became the friends and companions of famous people: Richelieu, Mazarin, Pope Leo XII.

But back to today. MAYBE, POSSIBLY, PROBABLY, humans can't do without cats. We are like you - we treasure independence. We do not think any animal is our superior, not even humans; but if a human earns our affection, respect and admiration, then there is no more loyal and faithful a friend than the serene, quiet and dignified cat.

You may have guessed that apart from the FAMILY and friends of MADAM's who like cats, I don't have a high regard for humans. CAT MEMORY and CAT HISTORY have made most of us very wary and that's why lots of humans think cats are unfriendly. Dad-Cat's comments come to mind. He said, 'a more unpredictable, unreliable, unreasonable, not always to be trusted lot would be hard to find!' and he was quoting from experience.

After all, humans are at the top of the tree but, and its a big BUT, how many of you spare a thought for those of us who are sitting on the branches underneath?

Cat Communication

Marmalady's sharp reaction had interrupted my thoughts about communications, so I shall to the best of my ability, as instructed by M'lady, try to explain how cats make their needs and feelings known.

Body language - perhaps that's the best description. We can convey with a twitch of a whisker, a turn of the head, a lift of the paw, the raising or lowering or swish of the tail and sometimes the 'roll-over' exactly what we are thinking, feeling, and wishing to say without so much as a whisper. We do, of course, make noises; we miaow, purr, swear and, if the occasion demands, scream. We also make what MADAM calls conversational noises that only cat-persons truly understand.

Littlechap has his special call for MADAM; Lita complains loudly, 'Meie-Meie-Meie!' if she thinks she's not had her fair share of meat scraps and MADAM always gives her more, (much to my annoyance). Ruff-Tuff has a way of saying thank you whenever SIR or MADAM have to open a door for him - 'Priumpu', and if he wants a biscuit, well 'Brum' does very nicely! I've noticed that Weed, one of the quietest of cats, has begun to make noises, rather like a mouse of all things, 'Eek-Eek'!

Purring, I know, is the sound most humans like to hear. When we purr we are saying, "I'm happy, I'm content, I've enjoyed the meal I've just eaten and I'm quite pleased to be 'your cat'. Did you know we call purring 'singing'? Did I hear you say, 'What rubbish!' But it's true, we SING! Unfortunately we're stuck with just one note but you must admit it's a pleasing, soothing sound. Certainly better than some of the sounds which come from MADAM's radio!

It could be that you think a cat is just a cat; but we can

be jealous, we can hate, be angry, be frightened, be happy, love those who care for us. It's such a pity that humans often misunderstand cat signals for that's when communication breaks down and we don't get our messages across. 'Cat owners' should take careful notice of the way in which their cat walks and talks and brings gifts. The cat could be saying, 'I like you, thank you for taking care of me, I'm glad I'm 'your' cat. Remember too, that cats have a special way of approaching the humans they like.

If you have a cat, when you come home does he run to meet you, rub round your legs, almost tripping you up in his eagerness to say 'hallo' and yet making sure you've been touched by either face or tail? Don't push him away - he's making contact, showing affection and marking you for his own. It's a cat's way of strengthening the bond between cat and 'owner'. You should stroke 'your' cat, rub behind the ears and under the chin, talk to him, show affection. That way cats become 'person cats' not 'place cats'. A *person cat* is a friend to the humans he lives with, but a *place cat*, well, he's attached to a place and has no real affection for humans.

Loving kindness means a lot to all pets and in exchange they will give unquestioning loyalty. Marmalady, Lita, my brothers, sister and I get lots of care and attention; I'm not so sure that other cats receive the same.

A thought has just come to mind; I can imagine you thinking 'WHAT A STRANGE CAT! How is it that he can explain so well?' MADAM was a teacher; so I am, in my opinion, a well-educated cat! Not that Marmalady thinks so; she thinks I'm stupid!

Oh, And I must apologise, 'your' cat could be a her, not a him!

Penny-Gelly Stands Her Ground

None of us ever thought that Penny-Gelly and Littlesusie could possibly get into trouble, least of all SIR and MADAM, but that's what happened.

Penny-Gelly was a quiet cat; she found it difficult to communicate with Dad-Cat and with her mother, Marmalady. It seemed to both of them that when Littlesusie joined the group that at last she had found a friend. They went everywhere together; if MADAM called 'Penny-Gelly' it wasn't just her who appeared, but Littlesusie as well. They shared the same sleeping box, shared food, went hunting together and both, more often than not, wanted to sit on ANDREW's lap at the same time! To say the least, they were inseparable.

It was late one evening; and only ANDREW was at home since MADAM had returned to her school for a meeting. Suddenly there was the most ear-shattering noise, outside in the garden. We knew at once that something unusual had happened; Dad-Cat checked to see who was in and who was out; to his surprise the only ones not in the Snug were Penny-Gelly and Littlesusie. At once it was action stations!

"Hoover, go out and check the lane. Hoffman, look round the garage, see if the light's come on. M'lady, Lita, go to the front of KEEPERS and call as loud as you can. I will go out the back. There may be an intruding fox. Littlechap, stay indoors."

Once again Dad-Cat had shown his command of a situation. We all scattered to do his bidding, even Marmalady. She knew he never asked her to respond to his command unless it was serious. I went at once to the gate, looked up and down the lane but all was quiet. The noise was coming from behind the cottage.

47

Hoff I knew would be by the garage so I walked along the hedge until I found my brother.

"Seen anyone or anything, Hoff?"

"No. Penny and Susie haven't been here but the light was on. Do you think it's that big fox we see sometimes? He's never attacked any of us before." Hoff was frightened.

"Don't be silly. He's had plenty of chances to have one of us as a good meal. No. We've had one or two wild cats around here lately and I think they've taken a fancy to Penny and Susie. Finding them is going to be difficult. Let's report back to Dad-Cat and we can start a search."

I could tell from Hoff's attitude he didn't think much of my idea but, if our sister and Penny were in trouble, it was up to us to find and take care of them.

Back at the cottage we found Dad-Cat in the kitchen and we told him that everything appeared to be normal except for the noise, and that the light had been put on by the garage.

ANDREW too had gone out and was looking round the cottage with the aid of a torch and had begun to make his way to the woods.

"We must follow ANDREW. The torch may disturb an unwanted visitor and if it's a local cat, we can see him off!" Dad-Cat made for the cat-flap and Hoff, Littlechap and I brought up the rear. Marmalady and Lita joined us; they hadn't seen anything but were convinced Penny and Susie were in trouble.

There was a lot of wailing coming from the woods. It sounded like a real get together of all the cats in the neighbourhood! We made our way cautiously towards the noise, expecting any moment to be set upon, but as no other cats appeared, Dad-Cat began to move quickly.

"I don't like it. Penny and Susie are in trouble; I hope they're not caught in a rabbit snare."

The thought of either one of them caught in a rabbit snare was most frightening. I was glad that ANDREW was there, he would, I hoped, be able to set whoever it was free. A few minutes later we came to a clearing in the woods and I couldn't believe what I saw in front of me, and nor did the others!

PENNY-GELLY WAS FIGHTING A LARGE, MALE PHEASANT!

Littlesusie was lying on the ground near by; there was blood on her fur and her tail looked bent. Dad-Cat rushed to help Penny and Hoff and I were not far behind. Marmalady and LITA went over to Susie and began to lick her wounds. Littlechap started to howl, he was so frightened.

ANDREW shouted at the pheasant, and the bird, seeing he was outnumbered, made off into the woods. We were very glad to see him go and began making our way back to KEEPERS. ANDREW carried Susie and the rest of us took care of Penny.

Once safely back at the cottage Penny explained what had happened. She and Susie had been out hunting mice, but unfortunately for them they'd disturbed the pheasant. He'd started the fight by flying at Susie who got the worst of it, and Penny had hoped that by making a lot of noise, we would come to the rescue. She could not have held him off much longer!

Littlesusie has a bent tail to this day: and Penny, she received praise and thanks not only from us, but from SIR and MADAM when they heard the story of her bravery from ANDREW.

Penelope - Pengelly.

Henry Cooper

I can't think why but the month of May seems to play an important part in the arrival of cats.

When ANDREW left school he went to college for further studies and the next year learned to drive. At first he was allowed to use MADAM's car, but after he had an accident and wrapped it round a roundabout, it was decided he should have his own transport. And that's why, arriving home early one day in May, he saw a tabby cat sitting on the grass outside KEEPERS. Thinking it was Littlechap he called to him. It wasn't until the cat was over the step and through the front door that he realised he'd made a mistake! By then, of course, it was too late to get rid of him. We objected strongly when this stranger was taken into our kitchen and given food, not that our protests made any difference and the cat did look thin!

"Stop complaining. How would you like to be hungry and homeless with nowhere to go?" said ANDREW.

Dad-Cat was most annoyed. "How does he know he's homeless? How could he let such a creature into our home? He's been in lots of fights and that spells trouble. He'll want to be top cat and I'm not having that! Not only that, he'll annoy the lady cats. Just wait till MADAM gets home; she won't be pleased. As that cat is in - WE will go out!" Dad-Cat made a dignified retreat through the cat-flap.

"As if MADAM hasn't got enough to do without looking after strays! OUTSIDE, if you please," said Marmalady; and we all followed her, most obediently.

Having gone, I wished I'd stayed for as we passed the study window I saw ANDREW using the telephone.

I found Dad-Cat and told him what I'd seen: "Dad-Cat, ANDREW's using the telephone. I think he's telling MADAM what's happened."

"It doesn't matter what he's telling MADAM; we will let her know what WE think!" Dad-Cat was going to show us who was No. 1!

As MADAM's car turned into the drive, we all marched down the path to greet her; Dad-Cat led the way.

"What's this, a reception committee? It can't be that bad, Dad-Cat. Let's go in and see what can be done." MADAM's words indicated that she was already aware of the problem, and as she picked up Dad-Cat, she said, "We'll go and look at the cat together, shall we, and decide what's to be done?"

We were able to eat our evening meal in peace. Dad-Cat told us that the cat had been taken upstairs out of our way but he didn't know what MADAM was going to do with him. MADAM and ANDREW were in the Snug and we could hear them talking.

"I'm going to telephone Mr. B. and ask if I can take the cat this evening. We can't keep him as he is and as the others don't like him, we'll have to find him another home."

I felt quite sorry for the poor cat. Was he going to be punished for being a stray? I thought of what had happened when I was taken to Mr. B.'s and felt even more sorry.

Henry Cooper, as ANDREW named the cat, came back from Mr. B.'s the next day and though MADAM tried to find him another home, nobody really wanted him, especially when they were told one of his back legs was shorter than the other! So Henry stayed. Several months passed. he tried to make friends with us and though we had some sympathy for him when he told us that he'd often been ill-treated and finally dumped outside our gate, we couldn't get on with him. Dad-Cat, who called him a 'poor thing', was usually kind because he'd known what it was like to be abandoned.

All things considered, Henry behaved reasonably well;

he didn't molest the lady cats, accepted Dad-Cat as No. 1 and understood that in Marmalady's opinion he was the lowest of the low! As far as she was concerned, he didn't exist! The rest of us, well, we ignored him as much as possible. He was a bit of a know-all and very pushy, like a lot of city cats and he neither did nor said anything which would've improved his position or changed our estimation of him. MADAM and ANDREW were always kind and loving towards him, but to us cats he was an outsider and could never be admitted to the group!

October that year was a cold, wet month and one evening, when it was raining heavily, Henry while trying to get home as quickly as he could was run over by a motorbike. The rider had tried to avoid him, but what with the rain and Henry's bad leg, he hadn't a chance. The rider was only a young boy, so he was very sorry for causing Henry's death. He wanted to get MADAM another cat but she refused!

I like to think Henry's last few months were happier than some he'd known; at least he'd had a warm bed, good food and lots of kindness.

Are you perhaps wondering how the cat got his name? Simple: we lived on Coopers Hill, he'd had a lot of fights, so what better name than - Henry Cooper!

Ten Is More Than Enough!

Henry Cooper's death set SIR thinking.

"Mrs. M.'s got some more kittens."

"I don't need any more cats to look after. Eight is quite enough!" said MADAM in a very firm voice.

SIR said very quietly, "There are two of them. Mrs. M. says they're going to be put down if she can't find them a home."

"I can't help that. She could take them to the RSPCA if she can't find someone to have them. It's quite expensive feeding eight cats and then there are the vet's bills and all the inoculations they have to have. No. I'm sorry, but no more!" MADAM was most emphatic. "I took in Henry Cooper because ANDREW let him in and that's the last to be given a home as far as I'm concerned."

SIR arrived home late the following weekend. Dad-Cat had been waiting by the garage to greet him and I was astonished to see him come through the cat-flap as if the Devil himself was after him!

"What's up Dad-Cat?" I enquired.

"If you've got any sense, make yourself scarce. There's trouble in store. SIR's brought a present for MADAM!" Dad-Cat jumped into his sleeping box and made out he knew nothing of what was happening.

I was filled with curiosity and was about to investigate when the kitchen door opened with a bang.

"I've told you I'm not having any more cats. They go back Monday morning. You don't have to feed them, train or care for them during the first few weeks. I know it's half term but I can find better things to do with my time!"

MADAM was very angry; her every action showed that she was not pleased with SIR. She did, however, put some food in a bowl and took it into the Snug. I followed, cautiously, and there in front of the fire were two black scraps, Mrs. M.'s kittens, one much smaller than the other and both looking lost in their new surroundings.

"When they've finished eating, they can go into the spare room. I'll get a litter tray and you, ANDREW, can take it upstairs." MADAM ignored the kittens and went back into the kitchen.

I gave the kittens the once over. They seemed harmless enough, though one swore at me, which wasn't surprising.

"Let me introduce you to your brothers, Hoover," said SIR. "Be gentle with them, they're not used to big cats like you."

I was pleased to know that the kittens were my brothers, because if they were allowed to stay, that would make their admission into the group easier, as it had been for Littlechap and Littlesusie. I decided that the thing to do was talk with Dad-Cat; he'd be able to influence the other cats, and if he showed MADAM he was interested, she might change her mind and let the kittens stay.

Dad-Cat was most helpful. He made sure that we all treated the kittens with kindness and encouraged them to feel at home whenever we had the chance. But despite our efforts to show MADAM we didn't mind the addition to the group, the kittens were banished to the spare room and only came into the kitchen at meal times. MADAM stated very loudly for all to hear, "The kittens are NOT staying!"

Saturday came and went, but by Sunday afternoon when MADAM had fed the kittens several times, she began to soften towards them, just a little. And once I actually found her stroking them!

Dad-Cat decided that we'd all take turns in visiting and I'm sure when MADAM noticed how often one of us would be

55

upstairs looking after the kittens, she began to suspect that something was afoot.

Sunday evening MADAM was heard to say, "I'll see if I can find a home for them. I can't cope with ten, perhaps one of the Staff at school would have them."

On Monday SIR returned to London, but the kittens stayed.

MADAM kept her word and tried to find a home for my brothers, but because she was insistent that they stay together, nobody wanted them; few people will take on more than one kitten at a time.

A few weeks passed and the two black scraps began to look less scruffy because they were given plenty of food and were brushed and combed regularly. Another week passed and then another. At the end of a month, when I heard MADAM say perhaps the kittens should have names, we knew she'd relented and the battle was over.

That's how my brothers, Ruff-Tuff and Tumbleweed came to be members of the group.

Henry Cooper's short stay had been of benefit after all. Nowadays Weed follows me around getting under my paws; if I go in the garden, **he** goes in the garden; if I go upstairs, **he** goes upstairs, and so on. As for Ruff - well he's a big strong cat, popular with everyone and devoted to MADAM. I think maybe when the time comes and I can no longer cope with all the duties of a No. 1, I might suggest that Ruff should take over.

Tumbleweed

Peter Podge

I was having one of my rest days, enjoying a little peace and quiet, when chance provided me with the information I thought I'd never know.

I've always been curious about the cats MADAM had before Marmalady. She's said many a time that cats have been part of her life since she was a little girl but I'd not known her talk about any cat in particular. Marmalady had mentioned the one called Peter Podge who'd been left behind in Belgium and that he'd had a brother, Simon, but that's all I knew until MADAM's sister came to stay a few weeks ago. She's also fond of cats and Littlechap and Littlesusie have a wonderful time; he because he's allowed to sleep on her bed at night, and Susie has cuddles all day long.

I can't remember how the conversation got around to cats but it was MADAM's sister saying, "I'm sure you're right, cats are psychic. Bimbo knew when Dad was about to die. He never went near Mother, I don't think he liked her and he'd never been near their bungalow until that particular morning. He sat outside Dad's bedroom, I couldn't budge him. I realised why later on when he came hurrying across the road demanding attention, then the 'phone rang and I guessed what Mother wanted and went over at once."

Those few words registered. Bimbo had to be a cat and of course we're psychic! How else did we get such a bad reputation as the familiars of witches. There are several things I could've told them if they'd been able to understand me!

I continued listening to the conversation with half an ear, not really understanding what was being said until I heard MADAM say, "I'm sure Peter Podge was psychic, there's no doubt he saved ANDREW's life."

That name jerked me wide awake and while I continued to appear fast asleep, I listened carefully to what was being said.

"Why are you so sure he saved ANDREW's life?"

"When ANDREW was only a few months old I used to put him in his pram for a morning nap and put the pram in the garden, leaving the french windows open. Podge, no matter what the weather, would go out and sit under the pram as though he was on guard! That particular morning I'd been making beds and having a general tidy-up when Podge came upstairs. He hated the noise of the vacuum cleaner and usually stayed away, but he didn't take any notice and just ran backwards and forwards to the stairs. He miaowed and miaowed so in the end I gave in and followed him. Podge ran down the stairs, out into the garden and stood by the pram. He continued miaowing in a most urgent manner, though how he could have known what had happened is beyond me. When I reached the pram and took a look, I knew that cat had saved ANDREW's life. ANDREW was still at a stage where he couldn't lift his head properly; he'd turned himself over, how I don't know, but a few more minutes and I think he would've suffocated." MADAM stopped talking for a moment, then continued, "Podge was a special cat, we all loved him and he was devoted to ANDREW. He never scratched him and put up with so much; there's a photo in the album of ANDREW sitting on him. I don't know of any other cat who would've put up with that."

There was silence for a while.

"Didn't you take Peter Podge to Belgium with you?" asked MADAM's sister.

I'd become so interested in what was being said that I forgot I was supposed to be asleep and got up. MADAM, thinking I wanted to go out, went to open the sliding door, so

I had to go into the kitchen and pretend I wanted a drink of milk I just hoped I wouldn't miss anything else that might be said. Fortunately MADAM went back to her chair and continued talking to her sister, I went and sat by her side.

"I didn't want to leave him behind, for although he was eleven years old, he was strong and healthy. He was flown out to Brussels in a special cage, but when we went to the airport to collect him, the man on duty said they hadn't got a cat. We knew he had to be there and as soon as I called out, 'Peter Podge', he set up such a miaowing that a senior officer came to find out what all the noise was about! Podge was so pleased to see us and ANDREW, well, he hugged and kissed the cat and insisted on taking him to bed with him that night!"

"Did Podge settle?" asked MADAM's sister.

"We had to arrange for him to have rabies injections; all pets had to have those and we had to keep him in for ten days. He was so good; followed me round the house as if he didn't want to let me out of sight."

MADAM stopped talking; I looked up and saw that she was smiling.

"He really was a beautiful, big cat. He had long, black fur, white paws and a fluffy tail, a bit like Ruff-Tuff. When the ten days were up we let him out, never thinking that he might be harmed. All seemed well during the day. Podge came and went, enjoying the garden, but when I went to call him in for the night I found Podge sitting by the back door, his face covered in blood. He'd been there some time; there was a lot of blood on the step." MADAM bent down and rubbed my ears.

"What did you do?" prompted MADAM's sister.

"Fortunately we'd become friendly with a Belgian FAMILY across the road and they very kindly telephoned for the Vet, who came at once. He examined Podge and said that in view of the size of the bite through the jaw, he thought the cat had been savaged by a large dog; he was surprised that he'd survived the attack and had managed to get home!"

I could feel the fur on my back standing on end; I was so overcome by the horror of the accident that I almost gave myself away and revealed that I understood what was being said! Poor Peter Podge, attacked by one of the ENEMY! My whiskers curled in sympathy.

"The Vet stitched the wound, gave Podge an injection and said there was a good chance that he would make a full recovery, but he'd be blind in the left eye. We didn't mind that so long as Podge survived. I sat up all night spooning a mixture of milk and water down his throat because the Vet had said he was to be given lots of liquid, and in the morning he did seem better. We all thought that apart from the blindness he would be OK. He had regular check-ups during the next six months and injections to help him eat. It was such a shock when the Vet eventually told me while Podge was having a check-up that he had chronic kidney problems and what was actually keeping him alive was his devotion to the FAMILY and monthly injections. He went on to say that when we returned to England, there was no way Podge would survive in quarantine, he needed to be with us all the time." MADAM stopped speaking; I could see that she was feeling very sad. "I looked at Peter Podge as he sat on the vet's table and I could see him as he used to be, a beautiful, healthy, lively cat. He was purring, so faithful and trusting." MADAM found it difficult to go on.

I jumped up on MADAM's lap and rubbed my face against her hand; I thought my presence might be of some comfort.

"I gave him a hug and a kiss and very reluctantly, asked the Vet to do what was necessary. He put Podge to sleep painlessly and he was buried in the garden in Antoinettalei.

Dear Podge, we missed him so much." Tears dropped on my fur; I didn't move but purred as loud as I could, hoping MADAM would know I cared.

"You did the right thing," said MADAM's sister. "I'm sure he understood."

MADAM stroked my fur and tickled under my chin. "He was as daft as you are, Hoover, and gave us a few scares, just like you." MADAM turned to her sister. "Do you remember when you visited us at Blindley Heath and we had that terrible thunder storm?"

"Yes, I do. I remember the water that came rushing down the road in front of your house and we thought it was going to come through the front door!"

"When Derek came back from taking you home, we couldn't find Podge. We searched the field and friends searched their gardens and garages, but there was no sign of him. We began to wonder if he'd run away because he'd been frightened by the storm. I'd just put ANDREW to bed when I heard Podge miaowing but I couldn't see him. It wasn't until we heard coal falling down in the coal bunker that we knew where he'd hidden! He'd gone in through the bottom opening and then as the coal fell, it blocked his way out!" MADAM laughed. "Silly old cat, good job he only had a few bits of white fur. It was some time before they were white again!"

Simon The Squeaker

MADAM and her sister sat in silence for a few moments and then, "Do you remember Podge's brother, Simon the Squeaker?"

There was no doubt about it, it was going to be my LUCKY DAY!

"Only vaguely. Freddie and I only visited your flat in Oxted once. But didn't you take him to St. John's Meadow?" MADAM's sister looked puzzled.

"Yes we did, but we didn't know he was a 'places cat'. Before ANDREW was born we were away all day and it never occurred to us that Simon would become attached to 'place' rather than to 'people'. He was always so affectionate, loved a cuddle and was ready to play games whenever we got home."

"When did you discover he was a 'places cat'?"

"After we had moved to St. John's. We kept him in for a week, buttered his paws, made a great fuss of him and Podge, and thought when we finally let him out in the garden that there was nothing to worry about. He came back when he was called but only after we'd called over and over again. He had to have been a long way away. Then one evening he didn't come back. We searched everywhere, around the house, in the fields; we spoke to neighbours, walked along local roads calling his name but there was no sign of him. Eventually we began to accept the fact that either Simon was dead or someone had taken a fancy to him. Then we had a phone call from friends who'd lived in the flat next door to us in Oxted; they'd found Simon sitting on their doorstep. You can imagine how pleased we were and we decided that as Simon had found his way back, he'd best stay there, and our friends agreed to keep him."

"Did your friends like cats?"

"Yes, I'm sure he was well cared for." I looked up at MADAM. She was smiling and I could see that her memories were happy ones. "He was a clever cat. He used to climb the tree outside their kitchen and then leap on to the window sill and he'd miaow until they let him in. I know why he liked going there, he was always given liver or kidney, never ordinary cat food!"

MADAM's last few words reminded me that yet again Ruff had stolen Susie's share of the liver scraps which we'd been given that morning. I just couldn't make Susie understand that she had to stop Ruff pushing in. It meant of course that I'd have to have a session with Ruff about his behaviour. I could appreciate his temptation, the thought of liver or kidney scraps made my mouth water!

MADAM's sister was talking again and her next remark really set my whiskers twitching!

"You used to do a lot of amateur acting. Didn't you use Simon in *Bell, Book and Candle*? Mother told me how well the cat behaved."

I couldn't believe my ears! Here was a cat who'd appeared on stage! I wanted to tell MADAM to get on, but she wouldn't have understood, so I remained curled up on her lap, willing her to go on.

MADAM laughed. "You know, I hadn't thought about that for ages. *Bell, Book and Candle*. Pyewacket, the witches' cat! You couldn't do the play without a cat and as I was playing the lead, it had to be a cat who would respond to me. Lionel, our producer, had seen Simon and suggested I took him along to rehearsals. Simon certainly looked the part; he was a sleek, black cat with white markings, very elegant. It was unbelievable how well he reacted: you'd have thought he'd been trained for the stage, he never put a paw wrong!"

MADAM stopped talking; she was watching Susie,

who'd jumped up on her sister's lap and was asking for a cuddle. I hoped she wasn't going to be a distraction. I wanted to hear more about Simon!

"How did it go on the 'First Night'?"

I breathed a sigh of relief. Susie's presence wasn't causing a problem.

"I was standing in the wings, holding my breath, watching Simon as the curtain rose. He was sitting on the arm of a chair, alone; there was no one on stage. He didn't budge and when the audience murmured 'Aah!' he preened himself, curled up in the chair and went to sleep. He just lapped up the adoration. When not on stage he was put in his travelling basket, and on the second night I discovered someone had made a big star, covered it in gold, shiny paper and pinned it to the basket! Simon really thought he was Top Cat; he ignored Podge for the whole of that week and for some time afterwards. We always referred to Simon as Pyewacket after that."

Huh, another Hoffman, I thought; conceited and full of his own importance. But as it is with humans, so it is with cats - takes all sorts to make a world.

"It's nice to know he survived. If he managed to make that journey across country, I should think he lived to a ripe old age!"

"I don't know about that," said MADAM. "We lost touch with our friends when we went to Belgium. He was a super cat; he used to give us some frights. Podge was never so adventuresome, he just followed where his brother led! I came home from school one day to be greeted by another neighbour in a great state of agitation. She'd been watching the cats investigating some nearby chimneys and was about to call the Fire Brigade to get them down. She thought they were going to fall in!"

"What did you say?" enquired MADAM's sister.

65

"I wasn't very polite, and told her to go away; that firemen had enough to do without worrying about cats and that I knew they could get down because they'd been up on the chimney pots several times."

"Did they come down?"

"Of course. As soon as I was indoors, I went to the kitchen window, which we'd left open for the cats so they could get in and out, rattled their food plates and there they were. There was a high flat roof outside our kitchen and Simon and Podge were used to playing there. They knew how to get off the roof and how to get up again and they always came and went through the window."

"Weren't you afraid that someone would break in?" asked MADAM's sister. "If the cats could get on the roof so could a burglar."

MADAM shook her head. "The kitchen door was locked and it had a bolt and below us was a very busy office and garage. I'm sure if the people working there had seen or heard anything, they'd have done something about it. But nothing did happen."

Littlechap came in at that moment and wanted MADAM's sister to pick him up as well as Susie. Their behaviour was beginning to annoy me; I wanted to tell them to go away, but I couldn't because I was supposed to be asleep!

MADAM was watching the way Susie asked to be stroked and cuddled. "Watching Susie behave like that reminds me of Simon; he used to do that. He'd roll over to have his tum tickled and then stand on his hind legs and rub his face against Derek's hand. He'd only do it for Derek."

I owed Susie an apology, she was being useful. But who was DEREK? It could only be SIR.

"I often wondered if Simon was a reincarnated goalkeeper!"

"Why do you say that?"

66

"His special toy was a ping-pong ball. He'd pick it up and drop it at your feet inviting you to play, usually at mealtimes. He'd go and sit under a kitchen stool as though the legs were goal posts and wait for you to throw the ball." MADAM laughed. "He never missed, always caught it in mid air and dropped it at your feet, ready for the next go. A lovely cat; a pity he was a 'places cat'." MADAM sighed. "Perhaps it was my fault but I'll never know now. But I do think Podge had the last laugh. In one of the last shows I did, a cat was needed and as Podge was more suitable for the part, he became an actor for a week. He played the part of Uncle Remus, but he didn't get a star on his basket." MADAM stood up and shook me off her lap. "Come on, Hoover, time you went for a walk. Soon be teatime and if you're good, I'll give you all a treat, some melts."

What could I do but go. At least I'd be able to tell Marmalady that she'd been right about a cat called Peter Podge and that he'd had a brother, Simon. I strolled round the garden reciting the names of MADAM's cats. I made it eighteen and Marmalady said she thought there'd been nineteen. Who was he or she? Perhaps I'd never know.

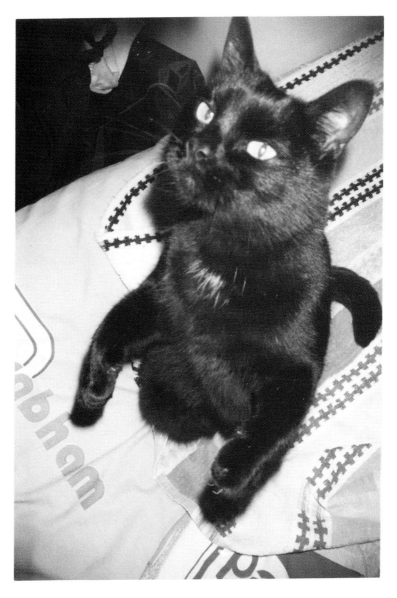

Little Susie.

I Wish I'd Never Asked!

KEEPERS wasn't a big cottage and ten cats more than filled the space they were allowed and there'd never been less than seven to my knowledge. What MADAM would have done if all the cats she'd 'owned' had survived, I just don't know! There would've been at least eighteen. Ten of just managed to fit in at feeding time, share the sleeping boxes without arguments, but eighteen - never! We could, of course, have called ourselves a CLOWDER. Did you know it needs twelve or more cats to make a clowder? Useless information, as MADAM would say, and she's always saying she has more than enough of that! I suppose that's what happens if you are a teacher; you store information.

Thinking about KEEPERS cats - we do have some unusual names. There's mine for instance, Hoover, and my brothers, Hoffman and Tumbleweed. Hoffman maybe, but Tumbleweed! MADAM's friends find our names very amusing, so I suppose there had to be some reasoning at work when we were named. I find it very difficult, at times, to follow human reasoning and thought. How is it that you can begin talking about one thing and end up talking about something totally different! But then, who am I to question human thought processes?

I can understand the reasoning for Dad-Cat's name: Rexie Dad-Cat, he was a Rex and a dad-cat; for Marmalady, the colour of her fur; for her daughters and son, Marmalita, Marmasetta and Marmaduke, follow-ons from their mother's name. But how did MADAM think up such names as Felicity Farnes-Barnes, Penelope-Pengelly, not to speak of Humphrey-Bumphrey, Timothy-Tuddle and Peter Podge!

I ought to have asked Marmalady when she was being

helpful, but at present she's her usual don't bother me self, so there's nothing for it, I have to ask Lita!

Lita can be so difficult. I knew where I'd find her; down in the orchard underneath the laurel hedge. Why she likes it there, in amongst the leaves, I couldn't even begin to guess. I'll have to ask.

Sure enough as I made my way through the garden, pausing now and then to sniff the morning smells and taking care that our boundaries were well and truly marked, I could see her white fur under the hedge. Already I was beginning to regret the decision that I'd ask Lita. She, I knew, wouldn't come out, so I'd have to go in! Very carefully I began pushing my way into Lita's hiding place; dead leaves stuck to my fur, a bramble caught in my tail and the thought persisted that I should have found something better to do with my time - but duty called!

After a lot of scrambling and swearing I reached Lita's side. She made a space for me, (just big enough), and miaowed a greeting.

"What brings you here on such a lovely morning? Are you feeling well, Hoovie-Doovie?"

She was obviously in one of her 'I'm going to annoy you moods!' How I hated it when she called me that. Putting it down it is bad enough but saying it!

"Marmalady's not too well and she said that if I wanted more information about KEEPERS and the cats, you might help."

"Do you mean to say that you actually crawled through the undergrowth just to talk with me? I am honoured!" Lita smirked.

Exchanging insults with Lita is a waste of time; it never pays off so I ignored her comment and asked, quite casually, "Why do you come and sit here? It's not the most comfortable of places."

"It reminds me of the garden at KEEPERS and my favourite place under the old oak tree, always lots of leaves to hide in. That's where my brother, sisters and I used to play."

There was silence for a moment and as I didn't wish to stop Lita giving me some help, I waited patiently for her to continue.

"I can't get used to the idea that I'm the only one left. I can't say to you or the others, do you remember when ... ?" Lita was full of self-pity.

Lita and I were not the best of friends but I felt sorry for her and I knew that if I gave her the opportunity of being rude to me, it would cheer her up!

"You called me Hoovie-Doovie a moment ago. It's not a version of my name for which I care but why was I called Hoover?"

The change in Lita's attitude had to be seen to be believed. "Oh, I know what's in your mind. You think you were named after the American President called Hoover. No such luck! YOU, you were named after a vacuum cleaner!"

I was stunned, shattered. Had I heard her correctly? I couldn't believe what I had heard. Surely Lita was joking?

"Are you sure Lita? I can't think MADAM named me after a ..." I couldn't say the word.

"MADAM didn't name you, SIR did. She named your brother Hoffman and he was almost called Dustbin!"

"You're making it up, Lita. Hoff said he was given that name because he had short, fat legs like a grand piano."

"Well, that's just where you're wrong! When you and your brother arrived at KEEPERS you were very hungry, and when MADAM gave you some Whiskas it was gone in seconds. You were given some more and that went just as quickly! You were both very greedy and hadn't been taught any manners." Lita paused as though she expected me to say something, so I

71

remained silent. "You didn't know the politeness rule, 'that you must always leave a little and eat it later'. You weren't at all well brought up!" Lita looked at me, hoping for some reaction, and got none.

"SIR said you were like a couple of vacuum cleaners and that he'd never seen food disappear so fast! It was then he suggested your names."

"Come on now, tell the truth!"

"I am telling the truth! SIR thought you should be named Hoover and your brother Goblin, as they were names of vacuum cleaners. MADAM said she didn't mind Hoover but didn't care for Goblin."

"Tell me then, how did Goblin get to Hoffman?"

Lita was enjoying herself; it pleased her that she could add to my discomfort and know there was little I could do about it.

"That's easy. SIR said that perhaps your brother should be called Dustbin as that was a good place for waste food but MADAM wouldn't have it. She thought awhile and then said: "I have it! Dustbin - Dustin, Dustin Hoffman, the film star - that's it. Hoover and Hoffman, those names go well together. So next time you're so full of yourself, remember you were named after a common vacuum cleaner, but your brother - he was named after a film star!" Lita miaowed with delight, very pleased with herself, her loneliness forgotten.

I sat up very straight and pretended I was quite unconcerned about what she'd said. "What's in a name, Lita? At least I'm No. 1 and don't you forget it. And all things considered, a vacuum cleaner is a very useful piece of equipment, more than can be said for a film star!"

How thankful I was that Hoff had never known he'd been named after a film star. He'd been conceited enough as it was, and that bit of information would made him worse.

"And do you know why you're sometimes called Boots?"

"No, but I'm sure you're going to tell me!"

"Well, you know Uncle Eric had problems deciding who was who and especially with your name and Hoff's," Lita paused.

"Go on, then." Lita really knew how to annoy me!

"So SIR said as you'd got four white paws, when Uncle Eric was around, you'd better be known as Boots!" Lita grinned like the proverbial Cheshire cat.

"You are a mine of information, aren't you Lita. Perhaps as you know so much, you could spare some time to tell me about Felicity and Charles."

"What do you want to know for?" Lita couldn't contain her curiosity.

"It's Marmalady's idea. She said that since humans think that because we don't talk or communicate as they do, that we are unaware of what's happening. So I've got to put down all I know about KEEPERS cats, how we communicate and are able to understand human talk. Will you help?" I watched Lita; would she co-operate? I was sure she'd refuse.

"What a good idea, of course I'll help! However, you must understand that I'm not as young as I was and I do get very tired, so you'll have to fit in with those times when I'm awake and feel able to help." Lita stretched and settled herself more comfortably. "I'll see you tomorrow after breakfast, provided it isn't raining." She closed her eyes and pretended she was going to sleep.

Where's the catch, I thought; what shall I have to do in return. Lita never does something for nothing! If only I hadn't needed her help, I'd have given her a good scratch on the nose to remind her that I was No. 1! Instead I said thank you and agreed to meet her the next day.

Lita opened one eye. "This time tomorrow then?

Delighted to be of service. Perhaps you could make a list of the questions you'd like to ask." She curled her tail over her nose and I knew that the only thing left for me to do was to leave her to think about what I'd said.

Hoffman

I walked back to the house, very slowly. I was not looking forward to the problems tomorrow would bring. Lita and I had always found it difficult to get along; two of a kind maybe. We both liked our own way. As I went through the cat-flap I was reminded noisily of my name; MADAM was hoovering in the dining-room. I wandered into the kitchen hoping against hope that there might be a little food left from breakfast but, as usual Ruff had been there before me. Lita had quoted the politeness rule, I don't think Ruff has ever heard of it; he never leaves a scrap of food and could still eat more! Where he puts it all when the rest of us have finished beats me. A click of the scissors, the rattle of a plate and there he is, ready and eager for more food!

I couldn't think straight. How was I going to deal with Lita? Why did she take such pleasure in being difficult? Why couldn't Marmalady be more helpful? Why was it my brother had been named after a film star and me after a vacuum cleaner? I couldn't get Lita's words out of my head. Film star - vacuum cleaner. How triumphant Lita had sounded. Worrying wouldn't find a solution but perhaps a rest on ANDREW's bed might help. As I went upstairs MADAM was still using the vacuum cleaner and I could hear Lita's voice:-

"You were named after a vacuum cleaner but your brother - he was named after a film star!"

Hoff would've enjoyed that bit of knowledge. Poor old Hoff; he would've been even more difficult to live with; always full of his own importance and thinking most of the time that because - in his opinion - he was MADAM's cat, the rest of us should sit and admire from afar! But I do miss him; we'd had so much fun together when we were kittens.

We shall never know what happened the night he went out and didn't come back. An accident, thought MADAM; a car being driven too fast.

At the time I found it very hard to accept that I wouldn't see him strolling up the garden path as if he was the only cat who'd ever lived at KEEPERS! Perhaps that was why I had given Lita the chance of annoying me. I could understand how it felt to be left; she was the only one left out of five and I'd been left without my twin. MADAM used to say that Hoff reminded her of Felicity and, from the time we both arrived at KEEPERS, he certainly made sure that <u>he</u> was the one SHE noticed. But there were so many occasions when Dad-Cat would have to give Hoff a cuff round the ear for stepping out of line, because he thought he didn't have to accept group disipline. As for me, I was ANDREW's cat and I'm still ANDREW's cat, though nowadays I have to look after MADAM, since that's one of my duties as No. 1.

February/March 1983 were very cold months. We'd had a lot of snow followed by frost and cold winds. SIR was away and ANDREW was at sea. We all kept close to the fire in the Snug and only went out when necessary; so it was odd when Hoff asked to go out late one night, just as MADAM was going to bed. I remember her calling him many, many times and then giving it up as a bad job as it was possible for him to come in through the cat-flap, and sleep in one of our boxes in the kitchen.

I thought he was daft staying out in the cold, especially when he could sleep on MADAM's bed in the warm! But Hoff hadn't been his usual self: bad-tempered, taking offence for no good reason, and quick to start a fight. Dad-Cat had stopped several set-tos between Hoff and Ruff and said he thought Hoff had found a lady friend and that there'd been a disagreement. MADAM decided to lock up and we all went quite happily to bed. However, next morning much to our surprise, no Hoff waiting to come in!

76

MADAM called and called, but there was no sign of him. Hoff was never late for breakfast. We wondered where he could be and we could understand why MADAM was worried, especially as it had begun to snow again. She put on a coat and went out to look for him. Dad-Cat and I followed behind and searched those places where MADAM couldn't go but there was no sign of him. The morning passed; still no Hoff. Even Marmalady and Lita took a turn in going out to look for him: in the garden, nearby fields and in the woods behind the cottage. They didn't think much of Hoff but they didn't like to see how his absence was upsetting MADAM.

It was getting dark and the snow had turned to rain when MADAM put on her coat once more, went out and began to walk down the lane. She was looking from side to side, searching the ditch and verge. I watched from the shelter of the hedge and then I saw her bend and pick something up. I knew as she turned that she had found Hoff but why hadn't we seen him earlier? MADAM began walking back to the cottage, carrying Hoff in her arms, I was so pleased.

I thought of how I would tease him about staying 'out on the tiles' and then I looked more closely. Was he injured, or was he making the most of a cuddle? Why was he lying so still? As MADAM came closer I saw tears running down her face, I sensed her sorrow and my tail drooped, my purred greeting forgotten - Hoff was dead.

Very slowly I made my way back to KEEPERS to prepare the others for the bad news.

You probably know cats can't cry, but we grieve and we are sad when one of our own kind is hurt or injured or killed, just as humans grieve over friends and relatives. We were sad to lose Hoff and it seemed worse because he wasn't be buried in the garden as we had expected. The ground had been too hard for MADAM to dig.

Dad-Cat was most concerned that we didn't know where he was and said, "Although Hoff had not been the most co-operative and obedient of cats, he was entitled to our last respects and a final farewell."

It was many months later that Marmalady found out that MADAM had taken Hoff to the Animal Clinic for cremation.

But some good did come out of bad. ANDREW telephoned from Belgium and on hearing the news used a weekend pass to come home the very next day and SIR returned the following day from his business trip. They knew only too well how MADAM would feel and could supply the words which we could not. All we cats could do was show our affection.

For me, the sadness of losing my brother gave way to the pleasure of having ANDREW at home, and I made the most of it. It was so nice to curl up on his lap and be beside him at bed-time.

Hoffman.

I Get The Fright Of My Life!

It was the uncertainty of Hoff's whereabouts which led to an unforgettable episode in my life.

I'd been quite sure that Hoff was dead when I saw MADAM walking up the lane, but later when there was no burial in the garden, I began to think I was wrong and so took to wandering off, looking in those places which Hoff had found interesting. There were several barns close to KEEPERS where he'd gone mousing and I began taking a look most days, hoping that Hoff might be around, but - no Hoff. I began travelling further afield on the off chance and once or twice I forgot to be back in time for tea.

Naturally that caused an upset and as Dad-Cat said, "It was a very thoughtless thing to do, especially as the group had not yet come to terms with Hoff's absence."

I was sorry but somehow I couldn't resist the urge to go on searching, until the day I got the fright of my life!

About a mile away across the fields was a riding stables in some old farm buildings and one afternoon, all unsuspecting, I wandered in and out of the stalls, turning over the straw, making a few mice run for their lives and leaving my personal mark in the hope that Hoff would smell it and know I was looking for him. Then, just as I was about to turn for home I heard a female voice calling, "Puss, Puss, where do you think you're going?"

Not thinking what I should be doing, I ran into a stall instead of running for home! The door clanged to behind me; I was in total darkness; A PRISONER! Caught by my own stupid behaviour. For a moment I panicked and then common-sense prevailed, though I had to admit I was very frightened. There was no way of escape; no holes in the walls, a stout stable door barring the entrance and a window at a level too high for me to jump, but also boarded over. There was plenty of straw so I wouldn't be cold in the night, but what about the person who'd trapped me? Surely she would come to find out if all was well with me.

Presently the bottom half of the door opened wide enough for a bowl of food and a saucer of milk to pass through, but not wide enough for me to make a dash for it. At least my captor wasn't going to starve me and though it wasn't what I was used to, it was better than nothing. I had begun to feel hungry and there was no point in adding to my problems by not eating; I would need to keep up my strength.

It became quiet outside: no human voices, a few muffled snorts from the horses and finally, total silence. I settled down in the straw, trying hard to sleep; but thoughts of how everyone at KEEPERS would be taking my absence nagged at me. How would SIR and MADAM take my non-appearance? It would be most distressing if I couldn't get back. They would have to tell ANDREW his cat was missing and his ship had just sailed for the Falklands. What was I going to do? How was I going to get out? The only thing, it seemed to me, was to bide my time, hope for the chance to escape and then RUN as fast as I could!

Try as I might, I couldn't sleep and later that evening I heard MADAM and SIR calling my name. They passed close by and though I miaowed as loud as I could, they didn't hear me and turned away, their voices becoming fainter and fainter. Many times in the next few days I was to hear "Hoover, Hoover, Hoover." How I wished that I could call out "I'm here, I'm here, shut in the stables," and they would find me. But although I understood them, I couldn't answer so they'd understand me!

Days went by. I was given food regularly by my captor;

she was very pleasant, but never left the stable door open wide enough for me to escape. Then one day she actually came into the stable to give me food and stopped to make a fuss of me. She rubbed my ears, tickled under my chin, stroked my fur and announced to my astonishment that I was now 'her cat', and that she was going to call me 'Snoopy' because she'd found me snooping round the stables!

'SNOOPY'! My whiskers curled in protest. Didn't she know Snoopy was a cartoon dog? What did she think I was? However, I daren't show how horrified I was as she held the key to my only means of escape. I began to express approval of my new 'owner'; I rubbed myself against her legs, purred loudly and behaved as though my captor was the only friendly human I'd ever known!

The next day I was taken into the farm kitchen for my food. I followed the young woman wherever she went, pretending that she meant a great deal to me, and showing that my previous home was a thing of the past and completely forgotten!

"Aren't you a lovely pussie-cat? Does he love his new friend, then? You're going to be a good pussie-cat and get rid of all the mice. Shall I get you a collar with your name 'Snoopy' on it," said the young woman as she tickled me under the chin.

A COLLAR! I jumped up on the table beside her and purred loudly, hoping that it sounded as though I was delighted with the idea of having a collar and I rubbed my head against her hand.

"You seem to have settled. After all, you know and so do I, that what cats really want is a warm place to sleep and plenty of food. Isn't that so, Snoopy? You've found a nice place, haven't you?"

I expressed my approval of what she was saying by giving a special, deep-throated purr. Little did she know what I really thought of the name she'd given me or her plans for a collar!

She didn't understand cats at all! You can't keep a cat unless it wants to be kept.

"I won't shut you in tonight, Snoopy. I don't think you'll run way. You've been here three weeks and I'm sure you'll have forgotten where you came from."

Those words pleased me so much that I made sure my captor believed that she was the only human who had ever been kind to me! Perhaps that night I'd be free. The young woman settled me down in the stall where I'd been kept for the last three weeks, but she left the top of the stable door open. I made suitable, friendly, cat noises, assuring her how pleased I was to be 'her cat' and she went away, quite happy, believing she was my new 'owner'.

I waited, curled up in the straw, pretending to be asleep, just in case someone came to check that I was where I was supposed to be. The lights went out, no noises from the horses; all was quiet. Very cautiously I jumped up onto the door ledge, looked to see all was clear and then jumped down and ran and ran for all I was worth! Across the stable yard, across the field, down the lane to HOME!

It was a happy reunion for everyone, FAMILY and cats. As MADAM picked me up she said: "Hoover, I'd given up hope of ever seeing you again. Where have you been? You're not starving, that's certain, so someone has fed you. I'm so glad to see you; I won't have to write to ANDREW, telling him you're missing. I've been putting that off day by day. Sir will be pleased to see you safe and sound."

I wasn't able to tell MADAM in words how pleased I was to be back at KEEPERS, but I hoped that my actions showed how good it was to be home with friends, both feline and human!

As you may have guessed, I don't stray far from home these days.

Flea-Bag!

How would you like to be called 'Old Flea-Bag!' Well, that's what MADAM has just called me. 'Old Flea-Bag!' How could she? I knew visits to Lita's hidey-hole could cause problems. I've scratched all the morning, more than MADAM finds acceptable, but its not my fault. Fair enough, I know we get fleas from time to time, but I didn't expect to get them from Lita! She's usually so careful.

There are cats, of course, who do not receive the grooming which we get: brush and comb once a week, spray for fleas once a month, general check-up, teeth, ears, injections, twice a year. I knew as soon as I heard the words 'Old Flea-Bag' we were in for a de-fleaing session whether we needed it or not! I shall be the first and naturally I shall have to set a good example, accept the brushing, combing and spraying, and, try very hard not to let that hissing sound upset me.

What MADAM fails to understand is that any hissing sound and, especially that from those peculiar cans she has, is frightening! Hissing is a part of CAT MEMORY. Haven't you noticed if cats are really frightened, they hiss. Humans think we're swearing, but it's one of our methods of defence. Thousands and thousands of years ago our ancestors and others like us were often tasty meals for the large and hungry animals who swarmed all over the place. We learned that copying the noises our enemies made helped to frighten them off; it didn't always work, but it was better than just waiting to be eaten! Young birds make the same hissing sound; maybe they learnt the same lesson. I've heard MADAM say "The best method of defence is attack!' As far as cats are concerned, hissing is defence and attack rolled into one!

Marmalady tells me that tabby markings are also a part of a cat's defence - I wonder if she's right?

Fleas are something we can't avoid; there are too many local cats who are certainly not flea free!

It's usually Ruff-Tuff and Weed who brings home the fleas and pass them on to the rest of us. I can understand that; they're still of an age when exploring in the fields across the way is exciting but that's when they come into contact with, as MADAM calls them, 'flea-ridden Moggies!'. Unfortunately, as I've said before, Weed has taken to following me around like a shadow. Why, I don't know, but before you can say, "I've got an itch", he's given me a flea! We've all got fleas, thanks to the pair of them, and we're all scratching. Then out comes the dreaded flea-spray and try as we might, we can't escape; Hiss, Hiss, Hiss! The hissing attacks and defeats the fleas. No more scratching? Don't you believe it. It'll be a short rest before the next flea invasion, and tomorrow I've got to visit Lita's hidey-hole again.

I wonder if you know the nursery rhyme?
One, two, three, mother's caught a flea.
Put it in the teapot and made a cup of tea.
But it won't be mother, It will be me!

MADAM's always on the look-out for something which will defeat fleas. The latest addition to her methods of attack is, would you believe, a FLEA TRAP. Now I know that fleas are not the easiest of pests to catch, but a trap! MADAM is convinced it will work. Only time will tell! I can't honestly say that I think humans are very good at solving problems; you only have to look around and about as I do, and taking into consideration contact with other cats, how can I put it without causing offence - humans solve one problem only to create another! No doubt you'll say, "What does he know, he's only a cat!"

I'm fortunate, the problems created by Littlechap, Ruff and Weed are easily solved. I have no difficulty in finding the answers. As MADAM says, 'If you want to succeed you need concentration and application'. I've got both, so no problems!

It's Raining, Again!

I hadn't really wanted to talk to Lita the next morning because her complaints of being all alone had reminded me of the loss of my twin brother. So when morning came I was very thankful to find that it was raining, yet again. Lita hates the rain and always stays in the basket she shares with Marmalady, and that meant I could put off our meeting.

I found her where I had expected. "Meet you in the garden tomorrow, Lita, provided it's not raining."

She miaowed an agreement and settled herself more comfortably in the basket giving Marmalady a push to one side as she did so. I heard the beginnings of an argument and moved out of the way pretty quickly before Lita could get me involved!

It seemed as good a time as any to deal with Littlechap who'd pushed Susie out of the way when she was enjoying her share of meat scraps, so she's been miserable for several days. As I searched for him I couldn't help thinking how like humans we were in some respects. There's always someone who's being picked on or bullied; in a group of cats it's just the same. It used to be Penny-Gelly, but now it's Susie; she's scared of everything and almost everybody. The way she acts only encourages her brothers to take advantage of her; I've told her so often, fight back, but it's not in her nature. She's a, gentle cat, always avoiding disagreements and loud, noisy behaviour. I don't like to seek advice but Marmalady might, if I ask nicely, agree to talk to Susie about her problem.

I sensed it was going to be one of those days when I wished I wasn't No.1 Littlechap was his usual skittish self; he'll behave for a few days and then he'll be back to normal, in trouble from the word go! Ruff had also been stealing food, but he was a little more co-operative. However, as he said, "If Susie leaves food and I'm hungry, there's no way I'll leave it! She knows she only has to say 'It's mine' and I'll go away."

Weed too, has to be found and reminded he shouldn't join in when there's an argument because he likes a fight; but I'm not going out in the rain to find him. There's no sign of it stopping and MADAM, who's been looking out of the window, has just exclaimed: "It's pouring cats and dogs!"

Now what's that supposed to mean? Did MADAM really say that? I shook my head in disbelief. I'm beginning to understand why cats refuse to talk as humans do; our methods of communication are easy to understand. It's no wonder that visitors from abroad find it impossible to understand what people say when some of the expressions the English use are quite unrelated to the matter under discussion! MADAM should know; she taught English to foreign students and often found explanations difficult.

For instance: 'little pitchers have long ears'. Have you ever seen a jug with ears and how are visitors from abroad supposed to know it's another name for a jug and not something hanging on a wall!

Of course 'leading someone a dog's life' and 'being in the doghouse' need no explanation as far as I'm concerned; but how about 'as brown as a berry', when most berries are red! Or as MADAM often says to me, "You're as daft as a brush!" How can a brush be daft and anyway, I know I'm not.

And as I have nothing better to do at the moment, perhaps I could bring to your notice some of the sayings associated with cats. I know cats at one time were not popular. Do we, perhaps, play a more important part in your lives than we used to? I think not!

Have a look at the following from my point of view:
A cat can look at a King.

Enough to make a cat laugh!
Letting the cat out of the bag.
Not enough room to swing the cat!
When the cat's away, the mice will play.
Like a cat on hot bricks.

I don't know any cats who've had the chance to look at a king and making a cat laugh is very difficult. As for mice, of course they'll play when the cat's not around; and what cat would be stupid enough to sit on hot bricks! As I've said before, human reasoning leaves me scratching my head.

And while I think about it, humans have produced some very interesting words using the letters C-A-T! Do you know why? Do you have reasons? For instance **cat**'s-eyes, **cat**'s-cradle, **cat**'s-paw, **cat**-gut, **cat**kin, **cat**-mint, **cat**-whin, **cat**-brier; and some very nasty ones like **cat**aclysm, **cat**apult, **cat**astrophe, **cat**alepsy. I'm sure MADAM knows, but she won't be able to tell me.

If only I could use words to ask why, or would it simply be better to **cat**erwaul in protest? Not that it would do much good, MADAM would just tell me to shut-up or go out!

And while on the subject of 'cat', how many humans will admit to thinking that an inn called 'The Cat and the Fiddle' got it's name from the nursery rhyme, 'Hey, diddle diddle'? Lots of you? In fact it was named after 'Caton, le fidèle', a soldier who defended Calais for the English! Not surprising I suppose, so few English people speak good French!

MADAM has just complained that she can't put the washing out because the rain is 'coming down in sheets'. I GIVE UP! Cats and dogs - sheets - I'm going to have a **cat**-nap!

Marmalita.

Lita And The Oak Tree

The rain stopped last night and this morning the sun is shining; so there's nothing for it but Lita's corner.

"You've made it then," said Lita as I arrived somewhat out of breath, having forced my way into her hidey-hole yet again. "Didn't think you'd come."

"I always keep my promises. I said I'd meet you here yesterday and here I am. Though why I agreed to this spot, I just don't know."

Lita sighed. "You didn't understand about the Oak Tree, did you Hoover? You think my affection for that tree is all pretence, don't you?" It was clear Lita wanted to chat before she'd consider answering the questions I'd prepared.

"Well, you tell me why I don't understand."

"I learnt to conquer my fear of heights in that Oak Tree, and learnt too that when you face up to things that frighten you, they're usually not as bad as you think."

Lita frightened? She always seemed so full of confidence and yet here she was admitting to having been afraid. My curiosity was aroused.

"I told you a few days ago that I used to play at the bottom of the Oak Tree, but I didn't tell you that I got stuck up the top. As kittens my sisters and brother and I had a special game. We used to see how high up the trunk we could jump and the winner was allowed first go at the saucer of cream we were given once a week. Of course Duke nearly always won, until one day I got so angry because he'd reached the highest point yet again, that I took a long run, jumped up the trunk and went on climbing!

"And you didn't know how to come down. What a

90

shame!" I couldn't resist the opportunity of scoring a point over Lita.

"You want me to answer some questions, don't you?" The look in Lita's eyes suggested I'd better be careful.

"Sorry, do go on."

"It wasn't until I'd almost reached the top that I realised there's a lot of difference in jumping up the trunk and straight down again and being up in the branches and not knowing how to get down! I could see Duke gazing up in astonishment and Penny-Gelly running round and round the tree, begging me to come down quickly because it was going to rain. I had to pretend that I was enjoying myself and called out that I'd come down when I was ready, and why didn't they come and join me. They'd no idea how far I could see!"

"Didn't any of them guess you were stuck? They must've known!" At that point I thought Lita was overdoing it; I couldn't accept that her brother and sisters believed she'd get down easily.

"Maybe Felicity had some idea that I was in trouble, for I heard her say to Duke that it was all his fault; why did he have to be first every time and that he'd be a nicer cat if he let his sisters win now and then. They waited at the bottom of the tree for some time but when they heard MADAM calling them for tea, off they went. I was left clinging to a branch, frightened to move in case I fell all the way to the ground below."

"Wasn't MADAM worried when you didn't appear?"

"Of course she was. Don't be daft. She and ANDREW came to find me and try to get me down. ANDREW even climbed part of the way up the tree but he couldn't reach me. In the end they went indoors and I heard MADAM say that if I hadn't found my way down by morning, she'd send for the Fire Brigade."

"But how did you get down?"

91

I was seeing quite a different side of Lita. I was beginning to understand how she'd survived being run over twice and being trapped in the loft for two days. She knew how to fight back.

"I got down more by luck than judgement. You see I didn't know that one had to go down backwards, clinging to the trunk of the tree, and in my efforts to go down head first, I slipped and was only saved from falling all the way by managing to grab hold of another branch. It was that fall that gave me an idea; I thought that if I jumped from branch to branch I'd get to the bottom somehow. So I began jumping from branch to branch; they went up and down like see-saws; sometimes I'd miss and fall to the next. It was dark when finally I reached the bottom of the tree, ran across the grass and in through the cat-flap."

"What did your brother and sisters have to say when you got in?"

"They were full of admiration for my daring. I never told them or any other cat until today how frightened I was. I'm the only one left out of five, I suppose it doesn't matter now who knows."

Lita's uppity behaviour had always annoyed but I could give credit where credit was due.

"You showed great courage, especially when you were only a kitten. Thank you for telling me and I mean it when I say I think you showed great courage."

We sat together in a friendly, cat silence; a most unusual occurrence for Lita and me! Just for once the irritation and annoyance which Lita generally aroused in me was absent and that would make it easier me for to ask for the information I needed.

Lita gave me a gentle push. "Come on now, don't waste time. You've got some questions you want me to answer. What do you want to know?"

And so I began to ask Lita to tell me about Charles Marmaduke and Felicity Farnes-Barnes.

92

Charles Marmaduke

Lita's agreement to help meant a great deal, not that I'd tell her so!

"Well, it's like this. I don't know anything about Charles Marmaduke or Felicity. I know there were two other ginger cats because I've heard their names mentioned from time to time. What I'd like to know is how did they get their names and what happened to them. I can understand why you were called Marmalita and the same for Marmasetta and the Marmaduke bit, but why Charles and what made MADAM put Farnes-Barnes with Felicity?"

"You lack imagination, Hoover. Just think about the names given to you and your twin. You know how Littlechap and Littlesusie got their names, and surely you remember that at one time it used to be Ruff and Tumble. Ruff because he has that collar of grey fur, and Tumble because he was forever tumbling about having a fight. Tuff was added to Ruff for the obvious reason that he is tough, and Weed was added to Tumble because, as SIR said, Tumble never seemed to grow like a normal cat and therefore he had to be a weed! The FAMILY only give a name to a cat when it has some meaning."

I wasn't interested in the names given to my brothers and sister but said thank you and asked Lita to continue. "Fair enough, but it's the Charles and Farnes-Barnes bits which interest me."

Lita sighed and licked her paws; she seemed unwilling to go on. I began to wonder if she had the information I needed. "I'm sorry, Hoover. It's not that I can't tell you, I'm not quite sure where to begin; I hadn't realised how sad thinking about Charles and Felicity would make me."

I waited patiently. "Would it help if I asked questions?"

Lita sat up, stretched, yawned and settled herself in a more comfortable position, "Right, Hoover." and she began to tell me about Charles.

"I was Marmalady's first-born and Marmaduke was the last. Of course MADAM didn't know whether we were male or female until several weeks after we were born, for that's when we were given our names. Duke, as we called him was easily picked out, he was the only male and as he had a large white mark on his back like a letter C, MADAM added Charles to the Marmaduke. More than anything else I do remember that he had extremely big ears and large eyes, so much so that he always seemed to have a startled expression on his face. Duke could never sit still for long; he'd be off, climbing trees, chasing mice, catching birds and getting into mischief and very annoying, when the rest of us wanted a quiet sleep."

"Surely Marmalady and Dad-Cat had something to say about that?"

"They did, but Duke never took any notice. When we were about nine months old, MADAM thought that she ought to find other homes for us. Sad really, but that's usually the way. SIR wanted to keep me, MADAM wanted to keep Felicity and the FAMILY decided they could cope with four cats, so a home for Charles was found with some neighbours and someone at MADAM's school said they'd like to have Setta and Penny-Gelly."

"I don't understand; if three of you went to other homes, how did I come to know Setta and Penny-Gelly?"

Lita smiled. "Somehow I don't think it was intended that MADAM should part with any of us, just as I'm sure SIR was meant to find you and Hoff and the others in Balham. First of all MADAM had a phone call: could she go and pick up Setta and Penny-Gelly. The cat in occupation had attacked both of them and almost killed Penny-Gelly."

"What did MADAM do?"

94

"She went at once. When MADAM returned, we could see that Penny was in a bad way, covered in bites and scratches and so frightened. She had to be taken to Mr.B. for treatment. A few days later I heard MADAM say, 'I'm going to see how Charles is getting on', and would you believe it, she came back with Charles!"

"And what did Charles have to say about that?" I asked.

"Well, when we had the chance to talk with Charles, he told us that he hadn't liked his new home. He'd been fed scraps instead of cat-food, he was shut out at night, not even a box in which to sleep, so he was very pleased to be back at KEEPERS. The neighbours told MADAM they wanted a cat to catch mice, not one that expected to lie in front of the fire all day!"

"Were you pleased to have them back? Brothers and sisters don't always get on well together."

"We enjoyed being together; of course we had our fights; what group of cats doesn't? Everything went well; we all grew up and became less playful but Duke never lost his restless streak; he was restless the night he was killed." Lita stopped and I thought for a moment she wouldn't continue.

"The first to go. He was in and out of the cat-flap, unable to sit peacefully and quietly by the fire. Marmalady became so cross with him that she gave him a cuff round the ear and told him to do one thing or the other, 'Stay in or go out!' Duke went off in a fit of temper and he didn't come back."

If it had been possible for Lita to cry, she would have been crying. All I could do was wait.

"We learnt later that Duke hadn't looked where he was going, ran straight across the lane and under a car. The people in the car were kind; they took Charles to Mr. B. but it was too late."

I remained silently sympathetic; there wasn't much that I could say.

"The driver of the car came back to KEEPERS and told

MADAM where she could find Charles. He was buried in the garden the following day; Felicity was the next to go." Lita seemed lost in thought and then said, "Marmalady blamed herself, but it could have happened at any time, Duke was never a cautious cat. He and I were the best of friends even though he'd play mean tricks on me. You know, Duke hated it when his name was shortened; He always insisted he should be called Charles Marmaduke and often wouldn't answer if we called him Duke."

"Did MADAM shorten his name? After all Charles Marmaduke is a bit of a mouthful!"

"No, and he was the only one who never had a nickname. Funny when you think about it. You're often called Boots, I'm Fat-Cat; I've heard ANDREW call Littlechap, Cheeky-Chops and I know SIR calls Weed, Wumsie! Even Marmalady gets called Ladybird. Do you think humans give pets and friends nick-names when they're really fond of them?"

Lita's question took me by surprise and I didn't know the answer. I had to be honest. "I've never thought about it; it could be just a human peculiarity. You think it's important?"

Lita didn't reply so I asked her if she was going to tell me about Felicity; it was clear from her answer that there'd not be any more information that day.

"Tomorrow if you don't mind. I know you've not done your Rounds yet and you must have a word with Littlechap and Weed because they've been frightening Susie again. You really should do something about their behaviour." Lita's attitude showed that she enjoyed reminding me of my duties.

I sighed, got up, stretched and agreed I couldn't ignore bad behaviour. "You're right of course. Littlechap can be a real nuisance at times and Weed, since SIR and MADAM have been able to change his attitude to humans and he's become a 'persons cat', is quite naughty."

"See you tomorrow then; same time, same place?" Lita yawned loudly, making it clear that she'd finished being co-operative, at least for that day.

I agreed that I'd see her as suggested and went away in search of a little peace and quiet, to lie on ANDREW's bed and think over what Lita had told me. Littlechap and Weed could wait; I'd had more than enough of their bad behaviour; punishment this time had to be of a kind they'd not forget.

Ruff - Tuff.

Ruff - More Trouble Than He's Worth!

Another interruption to my efforts to finish these stories as instructed by Marmalady! We've had a right scare this morning.

Just like Ruff-Tuff; no real thought about the consequences of his actions. In with four feet and hope for the best is his motto. It doesn't matter to him until much later that when he gets into trouble that we're all worried! But more to the point both SIR and MADAM are thinking that either he's dead, or that he's badly injured, can't make his way home and they don't know what to do or where to look!

SIR was woken up very early this morning to the sounds of a good, old-fashioned cat fight! On looking out of the window who should he see but Ruff, who'd stayed out all night, giving Gizmo, one of the cats from the sanctuary, such a mauling that even when SIR shouted and banged on the window the fight still went on. Eventually Gizmo freed himself and fled down the garden with Ruff in hot pursuit. Later when I went out it was plain that they'd been at it tooth and claw; there was fur everywhere!

Then the fun began!

Ruff didn't come in for breakfast and knowing his appetite, that was strange. SIR and MADAM called: no Ruff! They searched the garden, looking under the hedges, around the greenhouse and shed; no Ruff! I could guess at their thoughts; as Gizmo had rushed down the path pursued by Ruff, the post van had passed by. Had Ruff been hit by the van? Was he injured? Is he dead? Will we be able to find him? SIR went to search the field across the road, (not an inviting task since it's overgrown with weeds and brambles), but no Ruff. SIR gave up the search and both he and MADAM went indoors, not wanting to believe the worst, but thinking it must be so.

I thought of the time when I'd been shut in the stable and couldn't be found; how I'd heard them calling but couldn't reply. Several hours went by. If Ruff had been hit by the van and injured, then the chance that he'd be found alive was growing less and less. We were all wandering about, not knowing what to do. Should we go and search? Should we behave as if nothing had happened when I heard SIR shouting to MADAM, "Come here, quickly. He's in the garden!"

MADAM rushed to the dining-room window just in time to see Ruff disappearing into the orchard. They began calling and rattling our food plates to attract his attention and after some difficult moments, SIR managed to grab hold of him by his tail and carry him indoors. Ruff acted very strangely; he didn't seem to know SIR or MADAM, nor the place where he lived, nor his brothers and sister! MADAM made a great fuss of him and even defrosted some melts and fed him a little at a time, hoping that his favourite food would make a difference. But it was late afternoon when Ruff finally recovered and he began to behave in his usual reckless, bouncy, not my fault manner.

When peace and partial normality returned, I took the opportunity of taking Ruff to one side and asking him what had happened. He told me that the van had knocked him off the road, he'd hit his head on some stones and then couldn't remember how he'd come to be in the field. I reminded him that although I was sorry he'd been hurt, it was his own fault; I pointed out the importance of thinking before acting and that he should have more consideration for everyone's feelings - not just for SIR and MADAM, but for us cats as well! But with Ruff it's in one ear and out the other!

I have no doubt that in a few days time, when Ruff if

fully recovered, we cats will be treated to a recital of how he, Ruff, was defending our territory and if I wasn't able to do the job, perhaps he could take over as No. 1. He must be joking!

By the way, you'll be pleased to know Ruff has told me that he didn't come back immediately because he knew I'd be angry with him. A likely story; he must think, as MADAM says, that 'I'm as daft as a brush'!

I asked him did he really understand that his attitude 'tomorrow is another day' was unacceptable? Did he understand that his 'in with four feet behaviour' caused problems, not just for the FAMILY but for the group as well? Ruff lifted his tail and then thought, that what he was thinking of doing would get him into more trouble... and earn him a cuff round the ear!

Naturally Ruff's escapade has been very upsetting, so much so that I've had to cancel my meeting with Lita. She's annoyed although she appreciates the situation. We both know that it will be several days before our daily, uneventful routine can be restored. I've had to listen to Marmalady complaining about cats who couldn't be trusted, (meaning Ruff), who have no manners and no respect for their elders. She almost said 'their betters' but decided against it! Then Littlesusie had to be reassured and comforted; she worries herself sick over the most trivial of incidents. She thought that Ruff would never be found but then we all though that; and finally I discovered Littlechap and Weed planning to ambush any other cat who dared to come into our territory! I hope I made it clear to them that such behaviour was out of the question, because the last thing any of us wanted to deal with was a CAT-WAR! To begin with both of them wanted to have a set-to with me, but when I explained how distressing it would be to the FAMILY if anyone of us was badly hurt in a fight, Littlechap saw reason, and without Littlechap's support, Weed will, hopefully, ignore the sanctuary cats.

It had been been one of those days when I wondered why I had ever wanted to be No. 1.

I was thinking of having a quiet rest on ANDREW's bed when Littlechap came to tell me that there seemed to be a lot of activity in the guest-room. He'd had a peep inside because he'd seen MADAM going in and out rather a lot, but no one had mentioned visitors. Littlechap is very nosey; he's not called 'Cheeky-Chops' for nothing. I told him to go and play. I knew only too well what he might have seen and that could mean only one thing and, at that particular moment, I didn't want to think about holidays. Tomorrow, when today's upsets are less important, I'll take a look.

It's Cattery Time Again!

My suspicions have been confirmed! There are suitcases on the beds in the guest-room and we haven't got visitors, so that can mean only one thing - it's holiday time again!

The concern over Ruff's disappearance fell into place. MADAM would've delayed departure and all the arrangements which must have been made some time ago would have been cancelled! For a moment I wished that Ruff hadn't returned, then I realised that wasn't a very kind thought, but *I hate catteries!*

You look forward to your holidays, freedom to do something different, go where you've never gone before. But for us cats, we lose our freedom and we're shut up in a cattery. We understand why MADAM doesn't like to leave us at home. She feels that it's not right to ask friends to look after us and feed us, just in case one of us is hurt in an accident, but we don't go far from the house and we think it's unfair that we're deprived of home comforts.

We go to a good cattery and the people who own it like cats and that makes a big difference, so we're luckier than some I could name. Mr. and Mrs. A. know how to treat cats and want those in their care to be content. We are given two large pens, one for the lady-cats and one for my brothers and me. We have three meals a day, milk as well as water, and each pen has two very large litter trays for our personal comfort; and we look forward to evening rounds because every cat is given a cuddle before being shut in for the night and can retire to a heated wooden hutch with a soft blanket.

But, when all's said and done, it's not home.

I wish I had the power to make some 'owners' of cats change places with their pets and make them occupy the poor accommodation that's given to the cat. We can't complain, MADAM has always asked to inspect the cattery to which she has hoped to take us, but even she's been fooled once or twice!

It's so easy; you're shown nice, big pens with warm beds, told there's a choice of cat-foods, even put your own cat in personally, but *what* a difference when you've gone! Your cat goes into a cage, the food's not of the best, the litter tray's next to the bed, (and not always cleaned), and as for kindness, well! However, at the end of your holiday, you return to pick up your cat, there he or she is, in a large pen with all the comforts.

'Your' cat can't tell you, he doesn't speak human language; may I suggest you look the cat over very carefully. The signs are there; the cat's lost weight, is scared and wary - even of you, it's 'owner'! You might think I'm telling you a tale because I don't like catteries, but it has happened to us. MADAM would never have known, but she returned earlier than expected and found us in far from pleasant surroundings.

Do be warned. Have a good look round next time you take your cat to a cattery!

Now that I know 'we are going on holiday', I'll have a talk with the others and decide what we're going to do this time. Whatever we try we'll be found and put into baskets, but it does no harm to give MADAM and SIR a bit of a fright! Marmalady did manage it once; she hid in the field opposite to KEEPERS and wouldn't come when called. SIR and MADAM couldn't delay because they were taking friends to France, so they had to ask a neighbour to come every day, leave food and make sure Marmalady was safe. Needless to say, she's never had another chance to be so clever!

Last time it was my turn to hide. THEY knew I was in the house and I kept up my non-appearance for some time, but in the end I let MADAM see me peeping over the top of one of the kitchen cupboards.

I think I'll get Littlechap to do the disappearing act this time and I can watch the fun.

MADAM will say, as usual, 'they'll have to go in a day earlier, I really cannot cope with their vanishing tricks!'

Felicity Farnes-Barnes

Our plans are ready for next Friday, the day we are to be taken to the cattery. Marmalady won't join in, 'she says she's too old for such things' and Lita won't join in because she thinks it's beneath her dignity, but the rest of us will make a show of resistance. Why SIR and MADAM want to take holidays away from what I'm told is a very beautiful part of Devon is beyond me. Most odd, but there you are - that's Human Beings for you!

I was planning to maintain my normal every day activities so that MADAM wouldn't suspect that I was 'up to something', when Lita suggested that if I'd nothing better to do, she'd tell me about Felicity and would I meet her under the laurel hedge, so that's where I'm going - down to Lita's hidey-hole!

I'll have a good sniff round our borders and make sure our markings are there, but as it looks like rain, by tomorrow they could be washed out. I'm hoping it won't rain before Lita's finished, I don't enjoy sitting under dripping leaves!

"You know, Hoover, I really don't want to be put in a basket tomorrow and taken to the cattery. It's one of the best we've been to, but I'm getting too old for all this moving about." Lita was not her usual, perky self, admitting to feeling old!

"Come on now, it's not for long and MADAM likes to know that we're safe and well cared for."

"You could be right. Thinking about Felicity hasn't helped; she hated catteries."

"Stop worrying about going to the cattery; we don't have a choice. Tell me instead about Felicity." I knew from the way Lita was sitting that she was not convinced that all would be well; she got up, turned round and sat down again and began:-

"From the moment Felicity could stagger out of the basket

106

we had as kittens, she made tracks for MADAM. Though we were all loved and cared for, Felicity always seemed to get more than her fair share of MADAM's attention."

Lita sounded envious and, I thought, decidedly jealous.

"She was ginger and white, like Charles but had such thick fur; it wasn't long like yours, somewhere in between. She was a beautiful cat. If you want to know what she looked like, there's an ashtray on the window sill, in the dining room, with a picture of Felicity underneath the glass. What the rest of us found strange was the very good communication she had with a human, and if I hadn't seen it happen, I wouldn't have thought it possible. Felicity and I would be out hunting and suddenly she'd stop, as though she'd received a signal of some kind. Off she'd run, making for KEEPERS. I'd follow thinking something was wrong but when I got back to the cottage, Felicity would just be sitting on the doorstep. Within a very short while into the drive would come MADAM's car. If she'd heard the car I would have been able to understand, but when she ran, MADAM must have been miles away! Even now I find that very puzzling."

Lita scratched her ears as though she was still trying to solve the puzzle!

"Perhaps Felicity was more psychic than most cats." I didn't know what else I could say.

"No." Lita shook her head. "It was some special understanding. Lots of cars went up and down the lane but she knew if it was MADAM's. We could be indoors asleep, she'd sit up, go out through the cat-flap and there would be the car just turning in."

I looked at Lita and decided to remain silent and wait patiently for her to begin again.

"Felicity always sat on MADAM's lap; the rest of us would never have dared to jump up and she'd only make way for Marmalady. I've seen MADAM reading a book or sitting at a table, marking books, and Felicity would decide that she wanted to sit on MADAM's lap and get the attention she thought she deserved. She'd jump up, wriggle about and make such a fuss that MADAM would have to stop reading, or give up marking. She never got into trouble; the FAMILY just laughed."

Lita didn't say it, but I knew what she was thinking: 'Felicity had been a spoilt cat!' I knew too, because she couldn't sit still, that she had come to the part of Felicity's story which she didn't want to remember. I asked her if the leaves she was sitting on were making her uncomfortable, but she didn't answer.

"You know Coopers Hill was quiet, but there were times when people who lived in the village used it as a short cut for Bromsgrove, especially in the morning or late afternoon and the cars would come through very fast. It must have been the weekend, for I remember hearing ANDREW ask MADAM what time would SIR be home. Felicity and I were in the field across the way, when as usual she stopped, sniffed the air and began running towards the cottage; I followed. As she got to the lane she didn't check to make sure there weren't any cars on their way, and that it was safe to cross. She ran straight in front of a car and was knocked over. I saw her get up and go on running so I thought she hadn't been hurt. She ran on into the field next to KEEPERS and I quite expected to find her sitting by the front door when I arrived there a few minutes later, but no Felicity."

I understood then why Lita had been unwilling to talk about Felicity when she'd told me about Charles.

"Do you want to go on, Lita?"

"There's no point in stopping now. I waited, hoping she would appear, but after a while I realised she must have been hurt. MADAM came home and I tried to tell her that Felicity was in the field, but she thought I wanted to play and that Felicity was still hunting rabbits."

Lita licked her paws and pretended to be removing some dirt from her fur.

"I told Dad-Cat what had happened but as he said there was nothing I could do. They couldn't understand what I was trying to tell them. SIR and MADAM called and called but Felicity didn't respond; she couldn't. They went to look for her but gave up when it got dark. They started to search again early in the morning and eventually went into the field where I knew Felicity had to be." Lita stopped speaking.

"And that's where they found her. Was she alive?"

Lita was licking her paws again. "Yes. MADAM found her under the hedge at the spot where I had seen her go into the field. SIR carried Felicity home. Mr.B, the vet, came - he couldn't help. MADAM was holding Felicity in her arms when she died. They buried her in the garden next to Charles."

"How did MADAM take losing Felicity?"

Lita snapped at me. "How do you think MADAM took losing a favourite cat? She was very unhappy. Marmalady and Dad-Cat were also unhappy. How do you think they felt? Mr. B. tried to help by asking her to look after a ginger kitten that had been injured until a new home could be found for him. He wasn't with us very long. And then MADAM had another ginger kitten to look after, but he was killed just down the lane and after that MADAM said she wouldn't care for another ginger kitten. That's why SIR brought you and Hoff to KEEPERS."

"Were those kittens Timothy Tuddle and Humphrey Bumphrey?" I tried to turn her thoughts in another direction.

"Yes, poor things. Dad-Cat wouldn't admit them to the group and Marmalady swore at them whenever they came near."

"Odd names for cats; what made MADAM think of

those? Timothy and Humphrey aren't too bad, but Tuddle and Bumphrey - UGH!"

"I don't know how MADAM arrived at such names. You're such a clever cat - why don't you ask her? And before you ask about Farnes-Barnes, MADAM used to say Felicity was the only cat she'd ever seen with a turned-up nose and as it made her look 'stuck-up' she was given a name to match!" Lita got up, stretched and shook some leaves from her tail. "I'm going indoors, coming?"

"Before you go, how did Penny-Gelly get her name?"

"ANDREW named her after he'd watched some TV show, something to do with puppets. It was Lady Penelope, but the FAMILY had a holiday in Cornwall and when they came back Penny became Penelope-Pengelly. Why don't you have a word with ANDREW when he's home?" Lita's last remark indicated that her attitude towards me was back to normal, friendly now and then, but at a distance.

"Any more questions. If not, I'm going."

"No. Thanks for your help." I stayed where I was and watched Lita wander back to the house. She hadn't said it but I knew she'd had a fondness for her sister, even though she'd been jealous and envious. Lita had always been SIR's cat, but she'd wanted to be MADAM's as well; that much I understood. Just like humans wanting what can't be had! I gave Lita time to settle before following her to the house; there was plenty for me to think about.

Miss Bossy Boots!

As soon as I went into the kitchen to have breakfast this morning, I knew I was in for one of those days I wouldn't enjoy!

Lita, Miss Bossy Boots herself, is a first-class trouble maker! She thinks I don't know what she's been up to. Ever since I asked for her help with information about Charles and Felicity, she's felt more important than she really is. Her behaviour has become totally and completely unacceptable!

Ruff has complained that she stole his share of melts (though how she managed that when Russ scoffs his food, I don't know); Littlechap is ready to start a fight if she pushes him off his favourite garden seat again; Littlesusie is being subjected to a series of rude remarks so she won't come out of her corner; and Weed, he says if she so much as gets in his sleeping basket again, he will give her such a cuffing she'll not survive! The only ones she's left alone are her mother, Marmalady, and me! So there's nothing for it, but a punishment session; it's the one thing I dislike more than anything, but Lita must accept group discipline just as we all do.

MADAM's angry as well. She had to bath Lita yesterday; Lita found a patch of soot in a neighbour's garden and rolled in it. It took a long time to bath her, wash off the soot and dry her; it'll be some time before her usually beautiful tortoiseshell fur will look like fur and the white bits - I don't think she's got any, they look grey!

Her final act of disobedience was to tell my brothers and sister what I'm doing; Lita couldn't resist the opportunity of being the centre of attention. Since then I've not had a moment's peace.

Littlechap:- "Do you remember when I fell in a ditch full of dirty water and SIR couldn't get me out?" As if I'm likely to forget the mess he made when he was finally pulled out!

Ruff:- "Do you remember when the garden at KEEPERS

was invaded by a flock of sheep and they ruined all MADAM's roses?" Yes, I do, but it has nothing to do with cats.

That's how it's been all morning; thank goodness it's cattery time and that'll give them something else to think about.

Having dealt with Lita, I was just about to have a few quiet minutes on ANDREW's bed, when Marmalady asked me if she could have a moment's conversation with me. I thought from the look on her face it could be one of two things, either I wasn't living up to her expectations of a No. 1, or else she had a complaint to make.

For once I was agreeably surprised when she said, "I know Lita's being a nuisance. The best thing is to ignore her. She's decided to be more difficult than usual because I asked you to tell the story of KEEPERS' cats and the rest, and not her. But there's just one request I would ask of you, consider saying a few words about SIR, MADAM and ANDREW."

"I don't understand, M'lady."

"The FAMILY deserve some mention, don't you think? After all, if it were not for them and the care they've taken of us, where would we be?" and Marmalady walked away leaving me to wonder what had prompted that remark.

As usual Marmalady was right; but what could I say about SIR, MADAM and ANDREW.

I can describe a cat, talk about a cat, talk with a cat, fight a cat, do my duty as a cat, but humans - like us in character but can I, a cat, describe a human? I think not! What do I know of SIR, MADAM and ANDREW? What makes them important to us? It has to be the kindness, loving care, consideration, the acceptance that we are more than pets and they our 'owners'. We know that they are our friends and we are their loyal, devoted and faithful companions.

SIR works somewhere in a big city, MADAM was a teacher and ANDREW is in the Royal Navy.

Be satisfied with that, Marmalady.

Marmalady.

You Won't Believe This!

We're home from the cattery and ANDREW's home too. We don't see much of him these days, being in the Royal Navy, flying what he calls his whirly-bird, what ever that may be. He's brought MADAM a present because it's her birthday next week and so the FAMILY are having a sort of party.

"Are you going to look at your present," said ANDREW. "I've gone to a lot of trouble to put that little lot together. Some of the photos are a bit ancient, but I think they're all there."

MADAM undid the paper wrapping and there was a big piece of glass; underneath a lot of photos. "Where did you find them?"

"Well, when you were away on holiday last year I took the opportunity of looking in the cupboard under the eves. I knew you had a box full of old photos and I thought I'd find what I wanted and I did," said ANDREW pointing to a photo. "I remember Podge and I think this must be his brother, Simon, and there's the rest; we all know who they are!"

As always my curiosity got the better of me and without making it too obvious, I strolled over to where MADAM was standing to have a look at what she was holding. I couldn't believe my eyes! Whatever was under the glass was covered in photos of cats!

ANDREW looked down at me. "What do you think of that, Hoover? There's you, there's your brother, Hoffman." He pointed to some photos. "There's a good one of Dad-Cat by the front door and what do you think of this one of KEEPERS?"

What could I say? I understood, but would he understand me?

I looked at the photos - we were all there. Marmalady,

Dad-Cat, their children, me, Hoff, Littlechap and Susie, Ruff and Weed, even Henry Cooper, but there were three I didn't recognise.

MADAM pointed to one photo. "I remember taking that one of Simon and Podge when we were living in the flat and that's one of Podge taken when we were out at our allotment.I took one of Simon, at the same time. Do you remember, DEREK? I was always surprised that they never ran off. Did you find the one of Simon?"

"No, but who's this?"

"That, ANDREW, is Pickle. A lovely tabby cat, bigger than Littlechap, who looks like him. He was such a small kitten when he was given to me. I had to leave him with my mother when your father and I married, but as soon as we had a company flat, Pickle came to live with us. He was about six years old then; he was only with us for a couple of years." MADAM stopped speaking and looked at the photo. "That's when Simon and Peter-Podge came to join us. Ever since I was a little girl I've always had a cat to love. The first one was Father Mick. He used to let me dress him up in dolls' clothes and wheel him round the garden in a pram; your grandmother couldn't understand that I hated dolls, perhaps that's why she had Father Mick put down in 1940. She said it was because of the war, but I think she thought I ought to be interested in the things girls were supposed to like. I was given a clockwork monkey and she took that away from me as well. Not a suitable toy for a girl, I was told." MADAM went into the kitchen and changed the conversation by calling out, "What would you like to drink?"

That's it, I thought. MADAM's finished talking about Pickle and Father Mick, but I had to find Marmalady to tell her about the photos. She was of the opinion there'd been nineteen cats, but she hadn't known about the one MADAM had cared for when she was a little girl. 'Father Mick', what a nice name for a cat Perhaps she'd thought of him when she'd named Rexie Dad-Cat. It would be no surprise to Marmalady that MADAM's love for cats had started when she was very young; it's only when you are young that the extra special contact with cats - or dogs or horses, for that matter - can be made.

Twenty cats - what a record! - and to think sixteen of those could call themselves KEEPERS' cats, despite the fact that some hadn't been allowed to join the group!

I found Marmalady in her basket and told her what I had discovered.

"Are you sure, Hoover? And there are photos of all of them?"

"All except the one MADAM called Father Mick. You really should go and look. There's a photo of the cottage as well, and some of the garden and the woodland."

Marmalady went off to look and as she went, I heard her repeating what I had said:- "twenty cats, twenty cats' and shaking her head in amazement!

What Is Left For Me To Say?

We've been back from the cattery several weeks now and it's good to be back in familiar surroundings. It wasn't too bad at the cattery; as usual there was more than enough food, lots of attention and plenty of time to rest, but to have the freedom of the garden, the freedom to come and go as we like, to be, in our way, independent is of great importance. There are those who will think it strange, but we do miss being with SIR and MADAM.

Naturally our territory needed re-marking and we had to see off some local cats. Then it was back to the daily routine, until a few days ago when I began to cough and sneeze, only to discover that it wasn't just me, we were all coughing and sneezing! MADAM rushed us off to the Vet's, and much to her relief he said it was nothing to worry about; a mild infection and all that was needed was the right kind of injection. I can't say that we were pleased to have needles put into our necks, but the treatment worked and for that we must be thankful.

Then I noticed that Marmalady was not her usual, 'keep out of my way' self. Once or twice I thought she was going to comment on my efforts to keep the group in order and tell me, as always, that I was useless, but she just sighed and walked away. I knew then something was wrong, and it was for me to approach her.

"M'lady, what is it? What's bothering you? Is there something that I should have done as No. 1 which I've forgotten to do? Is there a problem of some kind?"

"No, Hoover, it's not that. All things considered, you've done quite well as No. 1. I never gave Dad-Cat the praise he deserved; it wasn't easy for him and I didn't help." Marmalady seemed lost in thought.

117

For Marmalady to speak of Dad-Cat in that way meant that what worried her had to be important.

"M'lady, you did your best; you always supported Dad-Cat when it was really necessary. Not all cats get on well together and sometimes we let our feelings take over rather than respond to commonsense." I just didn't know what was the right thing to say.

"Hoover, I'm an old cat, a very, very old cat. This last infection, the treatment hasn't worked. Because of that I must make sure that you are prepared for what is going to happen. Do you understand me?"

"Don't worry, M'lady, tell me what it is you want done." I listened carefully to the 'Cat Information' she thought I needed to know and hoped I wouldn't forget.

This morning MADAM had to take Marmalady back to the vet's; I'm prepared, but it's going to be difficult telling the others. Perhaps I won't have to, for SIR's digging in the orchard, next to Penny-Gelly's place and there can be only one reason for that.

Marmalady has had a good life with the FAMILY, loved and cared for from the day MADAM took her home to KEEPERS. She's been with them for nineteen years and she was at least two years old when she was adopted. This afternoon I will call Lita, my brothers and sister together and we will pay our last respects to Marmalady, a most superior feline.

What is left for me to say? Marmalady wanted me to tell these stories and now she's gone. You'll understand, won't you, if I stop putting paw to paper?

I've been told that all good things must come to an end, and perhaps the end is not far away. There have been times without a cat, but cats have always brought affection, loyalty and companionship into my life. The following is a tribute to the last ten, of whom only three remain: Littlechap, Ruff-Tuff and Weed.

Once Upon A Time There Were Ten!

Ten little pussy cats sitting down to dine,
One got half a tin,
And now there are nine.

Nine little pussy cats peeping through a gate,
One ran across the road,
And now there are eight.

Eight little pussy cats were going down to Devon,
One got lost at night,
And now there are seven.

Seven little pussy cats were quite the wrong mix,
One thought he'd have a fight,
And now there are six.

Six little pussy cats, very much alive,
One went off to fish,
And now there are five

Five little pussy cats hoping for some more,
One just scoffed the lot,
And now there are four.

Four little pussy cats went paddling in the sea,
One hadn't learnt to swim,
And now there are three.

Three little pussy cats didn't know what to do,
One said she'd go to bed,
And now there are two.

Two little pussy cats getting rather tough,
One didn't want to wait,
So now there's only Ruff.

One little pussy cat for comfort and a cuddle,
No little pussy cat to make the wool a muddle.

The Catalogue!

Father Mick	1933-40
Pickle	1949-57
Simon (Pyewacket)	1957-63
Peter Podge	1957-69
Marmalady	1971-90
Rexie Dad-Cat (adopted)	1972-84
Marmalita	1972-90
Marmasetta	1972-79
Charles Marmaduke	1972-74
Felicity Farnes-Barnes	1972-76
Penelope Pengelly	1972-86
Timothy-Tuddle	1976-77
Humphrey-Bumphrey	1977-78
Hoover	1978-92
Hoffman	1978-83
Littlechap	1980-
Littlesusie	1980-92
Henry Cooper (adopted)	1981-81
Ruff-Tuff	1981-
Tumbleweed (Weed)	1981-